Public Utility Regulation

Change and Scope

Edited by

Werner Sichel
Western Michigan University

Thomas G. Gies
University of Michigan

Lexington Books
D.C. Heath and Company
Lexington, Massachusetts
Toronto   London

Library of Congress Cataloging in Publication Data

Main entry under title:

Public utility regulation.

Consists of essays prepared for presentation at a two-day seminar held at Western Michigan University in 1974.
Includes index.
1. Public utilities—United States—Addresses, essays, lectures.
I. Sichel, Werner. II. Gies, Thomas George, 1921-
HD2766.P83   363.6'0973   75-2508
ISBN 0-669-99523-1

Published simultaneously in Canada.

Printed in the United States of America.

International Standard Book Number: 0-669-99523-1

Library of Congress Catalog Card Number: 75-2508

Public Utility Regulation

We wish to dedicate this volume of essays to Dean William Haber whose inspiration and encouragement have benefited the editors and his many other colleagues.

Contents

List of Tables

Acknowledgments

The essays included in this volume were prepared for presentation at a two-day seminar held at Western Michigan University during the summer of 1974. The seminar was made possible by a grant from Michigan Bell Telephone Company and was under the direction of the Inter-University Committee on Public Utility Economics. In addition to the editors of this volume, the membership of the Committee consisted of Dean William Haber from the University of Michigan; Mr. Lloyd J. Haynes, Vice President of Revenues and Public Relations of Michigan Bell Telephone Company; Prof. Barbara Murray from the University of Detroit (an author in this volume); Prof. William G. Shepherd from the University of Michigan; and Prof. Harry Trebing from Michigan State University. Their help in topic and speaker selection was of enormous value, and we are grateful to them.

Several other people were indispensible. Our man Friday was Ted Ferris, a graduate assistant in economics at Western Michigan University, who, besides chasing down footnotes, carried out such necessary administrative tasks as purchasing swim trunks for Walter Adams on the eve of his presentation of the paper included in this volume. Last, our thanks go out to four fine secretaries, Em Hollingshead, Sandra Laurie, Cress Strand, and Carol Myer, whose skills contributed greatly to the preparation of this volume.

W.S.

T.G.G.

Introduction

The period from the close of World War II to roughly 1970 presents a startling and dramatic contrast to the situation which today confronts both the utility industry and the regulatory community. During this period, both enjoyed an era of stability. Rate increases during these years were moderate, offset by rate decreases attributed in large part to technological improvements which resulted in economies of scale that produced generally lower unit costs. No customer suffered from inadequate supply of gas or electrical energy. Capacity reserves were good. A new generating station could be planned, approved by regulatory authority, financed, and constructed without delay and generally with public approbation.

During this period, the public utility industry grew and was looked upon as successful—if not especially profitable. Service was more than adequate by historical comparison or by the standard of other countries.

And yet there were forces at work whose effects are now becoming apparent and which have thrust us into a period of transition. Transition to what is not yet clear. Fuel costs have skyrocketed. Capital costs have risen by 200 to 300 percent. Labor costs have risen sharply and are expected to continue upward.

In the face of unparalleled demands for service, which in turn require unprecedented investment programs, the attitude of the investor toward utility common stocks is much less favorable than 10 years ago, and less favorable than both utility managements and utility regulators would like it to be. In recent months, investment banks have found it increasingly difficult to sell long-term utility bonds.

With this background, it is not surprising to find a general quickening of interest in the economics of the public utility industry and the economics of regulation. The subject of public utility regulation has received a fairly generous share of attention from economists, financial analysts, government officials, legislators, and journalists over the past half century or so, but there has been a distinct upturn in attention in recent years as evidenced by the published record. The quantity of research into problems of regulation, the attention given to regulation in industrial organization courses, and the space taken up in professional journals all attest to this growth in interest and concern.

Nor is all the attention in recent years of the same flavor: there is a relatively small group which supports the present form of utility regulation—and argues in effect that present forms of regulation are based on good theory and represent good practice. There is a much larger group of critics who feel that the theoretical basis is acceptable, but that the actual practice of regulatory bodies leaves something to be desired; in some instances this takes the form of asserting that the regulators have been captured by the industry, as illustrated by the recent resignation of the chairperson of a Federal regulatory body over charges of having become too closely allied with the firms operating under that jurisdiction. Last, there is a relatively new but growing group of critics who raise questions as to the theoretical desirability of regulation. These economists—mostly Chicagoans—have raised their criticism in two forms. First, it is argued by some that there never has been any sound basis for regulating the utility industry. It is alleged that the relationship between market concentration and competition cannot be derived from existing theoretical considerations which are based largely on an incorrect understanding of the concept of competition and rivalry. Then, second, there are those who argue that although there may have been a need and justification for regulation at some time in the past, in the case of many regulated markets and many regulated products the need for regulation has passed. Clearly, there are changes taking place in the market for public utility services which justify reviewing the need for continued regulation in the old fashion, with the old objectives, and by the old agencies. All these matters are fair game for the authors who contributed the chapters of this book.

One of our authors, Walter Adams, points out sharply that the essence of Schumpeterian competition is not price competition under which the consumer's alternatives could be designated in terms of marginal advantages in price between two identical commodities from alternative suppliers, but a much more dramatic process in which existing firms, existing industries, and existing technologies are displaced in wholesale fashion by new forms of organization and new technologies which strike not merely at the margin of profit but at the very foundations and the very existence of established firms. By contrast, regulation, according to Adams, tends to develop an undue identification with the industries under regulation—the power to regulate too often becomes the power to protect. Second, regulation seems unable to encourage innovation and invention or to penalize incompetence or lack of inventiveness. Last, that regulation seems unable to function without succumbing to the conservative biases of both regulatees and regulators.

Another author, Asher Ende, reflects on a similar problem but offers a distinctively different response: The basic issue in utility regulation no longer revolves around questions of money, honesty, and equitable treatment of customers. The focus of regulation in a fast-paced, rapidly changing technology, according to Ende, should be on questions of efficiency and cost effectiveness. The question should be not whether rates are just, reasonable, and equitable, but rather whether the rate levels, patterns, and structures are designed to encourage optimum and efficient use of plant.

John Monsees, the man who designs the rate structure for a large electric utility firm, reveals how it is done. He tells of the curious phenomenon of mistaking cost-based rates for promotional rates. Looking at different classes and sizes of customers and the costs assigned to serving them, he concludes that the indicated block charges, though cost-based, may look promotional.

In recent years public utility firms have become more concerned—voluntarily or otherwise—with pollution control and therefore with the formulation of accompanying investment and depreciation policies. Barbara Murray focuses on some of the relevant variables which regulators of public utilities should consider, specifically, what is the degree of irreversibility of the anticipated pollution, what rate of technological improvement can be expected in pollution control devices, and how the costs of pollution control should be apportioned among those who benefit now as against those who will benefit in the future.

Another of our authors, the chief regulator in the state of Michigan, William Rosenberg, focuses on the basic dilemma of rising costs and the resulting rise in the price of electric energy. Recognizing that at least 30 percent of the cost of producing electric energy is the cost of financing, he suggests a program of federal insurance and guarantees of utility debt that promises substantial savings. The great decrease in investor confidence following Con Ed's decision to omit its dividend payment in April 1974 can only be reversed, according to Rosenberg, by instituting strong national action.

David Schwartz is concerned with attacks on regulation. He carefully examines the institutional arrangements extant in the natural gas industry and concludes that competition cannot be relied upon to bring about good performance. He favors more Federal Power Commission involvement, such as in the case of "artificial gas" where the FPC has disclaimed regulatory jurisdiction. According to Schwartz, public utility firms have been attempting to shift the risk of doing business from themselves to the consumer. He argues that regulatory commissions should allow this only when consumers are also given the opportunity to share in the positive returns.

The responses offered—we hesitate to say solutions—by our authors in this volume vary widely, all the way from recommendation to deregulate as much presently regulated industry as possible to a proposal to expand the role of the regulator from a refereeing function to that of an active participant in the basic decisionmaking functions of management.

Overarching the entire volume is the Professor Boulding's wide-ranging criticism of public utilities, regulators, managers, governments, and economists, which ends with the restorative and encouraging statement that even in our unhappy present there is hope: ". . . I think we can very easily recover a sense of the future . . . a vision of what we have to do . . . to create a sustainable society. . . . I am quite sure that it can be done if we really put our minds to it and . . . catch a vision of it."

1

Entropy Economics

Kenneth E. Boulding

I have to confess that I have never taught public utility economics, and unless I have taught something, I don't know much about it. But public utilities have something to do with thermodynamics, and I have been fascinated with the way in which the famous three laws of thermodynamics can be generalized. They lead, in fact, to what I have called the "Three Laws of Practically Everything," because they do apply very universally. It is a little surprising that a rather pipsqueak part of physics could have produced these remarkable generalizations and concepts.

The first law, of course, is the *law of conservation,* and it simply says that if you have a fixed stock of anything, all you can do is push it around. A very profound truth—as Garrett Hardin says, there is no way you can throw anything away, because there isn't any "away." So whatever you have got, you are stuck with it, and all you can do is circulate it, just like the stock market. The second law, of course, is the famous second law of thermodynamics which is the *law of entropy.* The generalized second law is really that if anything happens, it can't happen again. That is, whenever something happens, it is because of some kind of potential for it happening, and that after it has happened, the potential is used up in some sense. In thermodynamics, of course, the only way anything can happen is by the heat going from a hotter body to a colder body; as it does that, the hot body cools and the cold body warms, and when everything is at the same temperature, nothing more can happen. This is why, of course, thermodynamics is the really dismal science. Economics is quite cheerful compared to thermodynamics because thermodynamics says, in effect, that we are just using the universe up all the time and that "this is the way the world ends, not with a bang, but a whimper." The end of all things is a thin brown soup with everything at the same temperature in which nothing can ever happen again. There is a third law, which I don't propose to dwell on, and this is the *law of approximation,* that you can travel hopefully, but you can never arrive. That is, you can never get to absolute zero, you can never get to the velocity of light, you can never really reach the limits of the human capacity to run a mile, because the closer you get to any limit, the harder it is to go any further. And while this is not perhaps a profound law, it is very generalizable.

In a certain sense economics is a subset of generalized thermodynamics. At least there is some sort of science of social ther-

1

modynamics. One of the things I have been going around advocating lately is that we get rid of land, labor, and capital as factors of production; each is an absurd classification of hopelessly heterogeneous clumps of stuff, and a famous example of a pigeonhole without any pigeons in it. We really ought to look at the economic processes as a sort of production function in which the three classes of inputs—and of course you have to have a holy trinity of some sort—are energy, materials, and information. I think this is much more descriptive of what the economy is like than land, labor, and capital. If we look at the economy thermodynamically, as it were, we start off with the second law. This can be stated in a great many ways, one way being that if you leave things alone, they will go from bad to worse. This is the law of consumption, which I sometimes call the "Law of Moth and Rust." Everything runs down. All of us here are losing 100,000 neurons a day. Even though you have a fair pile of marbles to start with, by the time you get to my age you may only have about 8 billion left. And then, as we know, clothes wear out; I will have to go and get another suit soon. Houses fall down, meals are depreciating, our dinner is now depreciating, and it will have to be replaced by breakfast.

Economic activities are a long uphill battle against moth and rust, that is, against the profound tendency of everything to run down. The way we do this is to put energy into the system to move materials around. On the whole, materials are conserved pretty well on the earth. We do shoot an occasional bundle off to the moon, and I suppose the earth has lost a little weight in the last few years with the space labs and all that, but it has probably gained some from meteorites. These are trivial additions and subtractions, however, and on the whole the earth maintains its equipment of elements very constant. In a material sense, all we do in economic life is simply to move the chemical elements around into more interesting compounds and shapes. In order to do that, we have to apply energy. Fortunately for the earth, the second law of energy has been repealed. The second law only applies to closed systems, and the earth, as far as energy is concerned, is fortunately not a closed system; otherwise nothing would ever have happened in it. The whole evolutionary process of which economics is the tail end is the process by which the energy input of the earth from the sun organizes materials and structures which contain increasing quantities of information. That is evolution, the history of the world for the last 4 billion years in a nutshell, and economics is just a continuation of evolution.

Evolution, of course, is the fourth law of practically everything. This isn't a law of thermodynamics, for thermodynamics didn't get that far. Fortunately, the fourth law is the only possible source of cheer. The other three laws are ultimately dismal. The fourth law, which is the *law of evolution,* can also be stated very generally: that you can wise up but you can't wise down, that is, there are certain irreversibilities in the process of information and knowledge accumulation, and this is really what the universe is all about. We certainly see this in social systems. Through some process which I still don't understand, the biosphere produced this extraordinary human nervous system with its 10 billion neurons. How natural selection ever produced us, I cannot imagine, because the plain fact is that the human nervous system is the most redundant and useless piece of machinery in the whole biosphere. We use only 10 percent of it now, so how on earth could natural selection have produced something that was so redundant and useless? The evolution of the human nervous system is a real puzzler. The answer must be that it came as a byproduct of something else. The genes are always going in for joint production, and I suspect that the human nervous system developed with long legs, or manual dexterity, or something of this sort, you see, just as a kind of accident. It was this other thing that led to the survival and development and propagation of homo sapiens, and the human nervous system just kind of came along as baggage. But once it had come along, it had enormous evolutionary potential.

Human history is the unfolding (another word for evolution) of the evolutionary potential of the human nervous system, and economics is, as I say, the tail end of that process, with evolution going into artifacts. On the whole, I would say that economics is the evolution of artifacts. Artifacts are a species; thus, the automobile is a species very much like the horse. The main difference is in its sex life. While a horse and a mare can produce another horse, a Chevrolet and a Plymouth can never produce another automobile. The real difference between social systems, between artifact species and biological species, is that the biological system never got more than two sexes, though sometimes it seems to have tried. The social system has hundreds of sexes. Thus, the automobile is produced as a result of the coming together in the womb of River Rouge of designers and architects, of chemists and engineers, of managers and workers, of lawyers and even economists, and all sorts of strange social species "mating" in a great economic orgy to produce the automobile. But the great evolutionary principles of mutation and selection and the principle of the distinction between the genotype and the phenotype apply to social as much as to biological species. In social systems the genotype is the knowledge structure, what Teilhard de Chardin called the "noosphere," that is, the whole sphere of human knowledge in the structure and content of the collective human nervous system as it exists in the minds of the 3½ billion people in the world.

Out of this knowledge structure come the artifacts. Capital, as I have said many times, is simply human knowledge imposed on the material world. The microphone into which I speak originated as a structure in somebody's head. Then somebody drew blueprints, I suppose, which are social genes. The gene was the first Xerox machine, except that it is three-dimensional, which Xerox hasn't got to yet. When it does, that is going to be an economic revolution. You can put your car (or yourself) into a Xerox machine and you get an exact duplicate out the other end. The gene was able to do that 3½ billion years ago, which was pretty clever. Fundamentally both reproduction and production are possible because of the process of the application of energy guided by information to materials. To revise Holy Writ: now abide energy, materials, and information, and the greatest of these is information, because of course it is information that guides us toward energy and guides energy to reorganize the materials. How much energy and materials we have depends on how much information we have. This is what development is. Economic development fundamentally is the human knowledge process and nothing else. It is just a process in human nervous systems and the way in which these nervous systems organize the world. The extraordinary process of development which we have had for the last 200 or 300 years we have been living through, even though it may be historically only a flash in the pan, is a process which originated in a certain acceleration in the knowledge process, that is, in learning.

This learning process begins before science, in a strict sense, for science itself comes out of the sophisticated folk technology of the European Middle Ages. In many ways science is a product of technology, as well as a producer of it. Thermodynamics is a good example. After all, thermodynamics is the theory of the steam engine. But the steam engine was born in about 1724 and thermodynamics in 1824, so obviously thermodynamics owed a lot to the steam engine, but the steam engine owed precious little to thermodynamics. Fundamentally the steam engine was Watt's tea kettle, wasn't it? The so-called industrial revolution of the eighteenth century was the tag end of a long improvement in folk technology in the European Middle Ages. Then out of this comes the scientific revolution, and out of that comes the huge technological upsurge of science-based technology since about 1860. I have argued that the Great Age of Change was my grandfather's life really, about 1860 to 1920. I have not seen as much change as he did, certainly not in the technical sense. As I look back on my boyhood in Liverpool in the twenties, we had electric lights, we had telephones, we had automobiles, we had our first radio when I was twelve, we knew how to fly, we had steel-frame buildings; fundamentally I grew up in the modern world, and what I have seen in my lifetime has been more of the same. I have seen a few changes, like television, which is more important culturally as a substitute for grandmother than it is technologically.

I have seen some rather fundamental social changes, such as the aristocratization of the middle class, which is the sexual revolution, and, of course, I have seen a very real "mondialization" of culture; in a sense I have seen the disappearance of the exotic. As I look back on my undergraduate days at Oxford, it really seems like a medieval finishing school: Classics and Western Civ. still dominated it. If you go to the University of Michigan today, you will find good Greek and Latin, but it also teaches Arabic, Urdu, and Hindi; Swahili, I think went to East Lansing, but Chinese, Japanese, and Korean are taught. In a sense, all our big universities are now world universities. This is, of course, why the states don't want to pay for them. I can hardly blame them for that. This is very real change, but as far as technical change goes, I feel I have not seen all that much, and my children may see less.

Where, then, are we now? This is a very critical question, for we are perhaps at a very critical moment in human history. I read a fascinating book a few months ago by an Englishman, John Wilkinson, called *Poverty and Progress,* in which he argues essentially that the development of the human race follows a constant pattern in which population control breaks down. The human group then expands to the limits of its existing technological niche, and either this creates disaster, as it did, for instance, in the Mayan or the Khmer civilization, or else it produces a breakthrough into another knowledge system, another technology, and an expansion of the human niche. Thus, we see the history of the human race as a succession of niche expansions as a result of the increasing knowledge structure. We begin, of course, with the Paleolithic and improved tools; then comes agriculture—that produces an enormous niche expansion; then metallurgy; in the last 200 or 300 years the scientific revolution produced an enormous niche expansion. On the other hand, it certainly looks like the population is now expanding up to the limits of the enlarged niche, and the question is whether a further niche expansion is possible. Well, maybe not; maybe this is the last niche of the human race. When we get to 10 billion, maybe that is as far as we can possibly go. We cannot be quite sure of this, but at least it isn't wholly implausible that we are now expanding into our final niche. Even with further possibilities of niche expansion it would be very hard for us to go to a 100 billion or 1 trillion people.

Is this, then, the ultimate Malthusian crisis? Up to now the Malthusian crises have always been put off, for the last 500,000 years, by the expansion of the niche. But now, perhaps, the niche is not expandable any more. I don't think we are going into outer space; that is, the thing revealed by the space enterprises is that the earth is the only decent piece of real estate for a very long distance. We certainly are not going to populate the solar system, and I do not think we're going to the stars, just because of the communications problem. At least if we do, we will simply shoot people off and kiss them goodbye and never see them again. Space colonization is too expensive to be plausible. I think we are stuck with a society and an economy which is not presently sustainable; that is, our existing technology is intrinsically suicidal, insofar as it is based on exhaustible resources. One of the fundamental principles of the world is that if you go on using exhaustible resources, eventually they will be all gone. This is almost all there is behind the Club of Rome projections.

It is true, of course, that in the past we have expanded resources very substantially by new knowledge, and we will continue to do so. The major weakness of the Forrester analysis is precisely its assumption that natural resources are a bathtub with a drain but no faucet, whereas in the last 100 years natural resources have had an enormous faucet. We have increased natural resources tremendously through the increase of knowledge. We didn't have oil 115 years ago. When was the first oil well discovered, 1859 wasn't it? Thirty years ago we didn't have uranium. Now we don't have deuterium, but maybe we will. Certainly, if we go to fusion, the raw materials are plentiful; no doubt of that. On the other hand, we still have what I call a linear economy which goes from oil wells, coal mines, and iron ore mines, through commodities, replacing what decays (and doing more than that if you have development, so that you increase the total stock), and then it all goes out into garbage. The ultimate product of economic life is garbage. So if we go on this way, eventually either we run out of mines or we run out of pollutables. The only possible sustainable society is one that circulates its materials, which turns the garbage dumps into mines.

The ultimate sustainable society also has to rely on solar energy. We cannot even rely on fusion for more than 500,000 years, and we have had 500,000 years of humanity already, so that is not really so long. In any case, if we go in for fusion, then in 10,000 years we may melt the icecaps because of released heat. If we go on burning up our spaceship, we will heat it up; there is no way of getting out of that one. The heat balance of the earth is a very precarious, sensitive balance. The truth is that the earth is a very complex, precarious system about which we know very little. When it comes to the study of the earth as a total system, the natural sciences seem backward in comparison to the social sciences. Economists usually know whether we are having an inflation or deflation, even if we don't know what to do about it. The meteorologists don't even seem to know whether the earth is cooling down or warming up. Five years ago it was all the greenhouse effect, the icecaps were going to melt, and that would turn New York into a Venice, which would be charming, for then the ocean levels would rise 180 feet. We are all petrified about the new Ice Age. The decline in world temperature in the last five years is unprecedented, and if this goes on, the ice will come down on Michigan in 25 years. Last year the area of permanent ice and snow increased 10 percent. This is frightening. If the Ice Age reaches the equator, that will be the end of us. But of one thing we are quite sure: the human race did not cause the last Ice Age. There just were not enough of us around. The earth is in the grip of enormous systems which we do not understand at all, systems in which the human race is still just a pipsqueak.

Nevertheless, a major criterion for judging any social policy of the present era is whether it makes the achievement of a reasonably sustainable society more or less probable. The probability is by no means 100 percent. The human race may easily be an unsuccessful experiment in evolution, and perhaps the octopuses will take over. As a matter of fact, the whole earth may be an unsuccessful experiment in evolution. It has only been going 3½ billion years, and that is not very long, compared to eternity. For all we know, evolution may be grinding to a grand climax, and we have no guarantee that the human race is the last word. Nevertheless, I have race prejudice about the human race. I am in favor of it, and even if we produce our evolutionary successor, I won't like him, or her, or it, whatever it is. What makes me an optimist is knowing that we have not exhausted the evolutionary potential of the human nervous system. If we're only using 10 percent of our capacity, there must be something ahead. Our capacity for problem-solving, for mutation, and for learning is by no means exhausted, and the fourth law is the cheerful one. Evolution must be possible, because it happened. It even has a certain sense of direction, and I would not even mind confessing to a naive nineteenth-century belief in progress; that is, I think there are times when things go from worse to better rather than from better to worse.

Now I suppose I ought to say something about public utilities, even if I don't know much about them. I have just been reading the Ford Foundation Energy Policy Project draft report. It is an interesting document. It may be wrong in parts, but at least it is not bland. I am quite sure it will rouse a good deal of controversy. It proposes three "scenarios" which spotlight a possible continuum of images of the future. One scenario is "business as usual"; that is, we just go on growing in energy consumption as we have been doing. We can do this for another generation, though probably not for two generations. We can do it until the year 2000, and by then we will have used up most of our potential, and we certainly will not have very much freedom of action.

The second scenario the report calls the "technical fix," which I think is a poor name for it; I would call it the "good housekeeping" scenario. This is good old New England prudence and providence. To be provident, we should go in very heavily for energy savings, which we certainly can do. There is a very large potential for the economizing of energy without hurting anybody very much. We have not done very much of this in the past because energy has been so fantastically cheap. If something is cheap, you do not have to economize it, obviously. So it has been quite rational in a certain sense not to economize energy, for it has been cheaper to use it wastefully. But, of course, if it becomes scarcer and dearer, then it begins to pay to economize it, and the report points out quite rightly that there are large technical possibilities here. It's a nice question, however, as to who is going to do it. It is one of the gravest weaknesses of our society and of other developed societies that we had growth for so long that all our institutions, our habits of thinking, and our education patterns have survived because they have been well adapted to growth. Now, since we suddenly no longer have growth, then obviously many of our institutions are very badly adapted to the new situation.

The universities are a good illustration of this problem. My own university has not grown now, thanks to the state legislature, for about four years, and we find that ZPG is not all that pleasant. In a no-growth university you cannot get anything new without getting rid of something old, and around a university this is very, very difficult. So we find ourselves stuck in existing patterns. The morale of the institution has decayed, and relations among the faculty and between the faculty and the administration have deteriorated. In fact, if it were not for the marvelous placidity and conservatism of the students, the whole place might fall apart. As it is, there is a real failure of adaptation to a cessation of growth. This is a particularly severe problem for American society, because we are so well adapted to growth. We are going to have to do some very hard thinking toward adapting our institutions to slow growth, no growth, or even decline. I do not expect "no growth" for at least another generation, but I do expect a period of slower growth than we have had over the last 100 years, as we expand toward the limits of our niche.

The third scenario of the Ford report is zero energy growth by the year 2000. Perhaps this is a little extreme. All sorts of technical things could upset this, like fusion, or even a real breakthrough on solar energy. The whole biosphere uses less than 1 percent of the solar energy that falls on the earth. If we could get this up to 2 percent, it might be all we need. My private solution to the energy crisis is sugar. This is a beautiful energy converter. You can make alcohol out of it, and you can burn the alcohol. If we start breeding plants for energy conversion, substantial increase in yields might be feasible. There are all sorts of technical potentials which could upset all the predictions of the doomsayers. I am a firm believer in the principle that all predictions are wrong, including mine. I have little faith in predictions of the future, and less faith in any plans which are built on them. The safest way to prepare for the future is to prepare to be surprised, as you surely will be.

If you look at the social system as an evolutionary system, it is the meek who inherit the earth. The race is not for the strong. Strength means adaptation, and adaptation is a recipe for extinction. The recipe for survival is adaptability, and adaptability is often competitive with adaptation. This is one of the puzzles of evolutionary theory, as to how or why anything survived, because you have to be adapted to survive in the short run, you have to be adaptable to survive in the long run, and adaptation and adaptability are often alternatives. That is an extraordinary puzzle about evolutionary theory.

Where, then, does all this theory leave the utilities? I don't know. But I suspect it raises a lot of questions which have not been asked very much before—such as, what role are the utilities going to play in the dynamics of human survival, that is, in the development of a sustainable society? Part of the answer to this depends on the relative price of energy. As an economist I am a great believer in the virtues of dearness. I was once on a committee that was supposed to advise the state of California on its water policy. Unfortunately, when the California legislature discovered what the committee was going to say, they abolished it before we could say anything. Our view was that Californians were out of their minds. If you had something like water which is plentiful now, but is going to be scarce later, then the thing to do is to tax the daylights out of it now. Our proposal was for about a tenfold tax on water. It is a perfect thing to tax. A water tax would be progressive, as the rich use much more then the poor, and such a tax would in effect encourage water-saving improvements. If anything is cheap, we are unlikely to have any economizing improvements.

Like water, energy is plentiful now and may be scarce later. If that is so, it is important *now* to make energy dear, and then we will get energy-conserving improvements. The Arabs have been very helpful about this. They have done us a real good turn, which they didn't intend, because they have forced us to think about something now which otherwise we might not have thought about until it was too late. Well, I'm afraid we've begun to stop thinking about it, but I hope that we go on thinking about it. But certainly a rise in the price of energy seems like a good strategy. One of my theories of how you ought to distort the relative price structure is that you ought to try to anticipate the relative price structure 25 years from now, because this is the way you will produce an offset to the changes, the undesirable changes especially, which are going to take place. That is, if we want to have plentiful energy in the twenty-first century, we had better make it expensive now, and then we will conserve it.

Now, however, we run into the great dilemma of economics, that is, how to make something expensive without making a lot of lucky bastards rich. This is the great dilemma between allocation and distribution. If you just allow the old neoclassical system to take its course, then you are extremely likely to run into adverse distributional effects. This is probably the most severe problem which is facing us, especially on a world scale. Dear energy is okay for our great grandchildren, but it's pretty rough on

India now. The whole developmental enterprise in the tropics in the last 25 years could easily lead to an unprecedented disaster. We have encouraged these people to go in for fancy new wheats and rice which depend on fertilizers and energy, and then maybe there is not going to be enough. Then we could have the Irish famine of 1846 all over again on a much larger scale. The Irish famine was a nice example of the failure of an early process of technical aid. The Irish were living in misery on barley in the 1700s. Then somebody introduced the potato in an early Point Four Program, and this led to an appalling disaster in about 1846. In the absence of some sort of total system which can prevent the human race from expanding into its ultimate niche, it is hard to evade what I have called the "Utterly Dismal Theorem." This is the proposition that if the only thing that can check the growth of a human population is starvation and misery, any improvement will enable a larger number of people to be miserable, so that any technical improvement increases the amount of human misery. There have been enough examples of this that we cannot simply brush it off.

How, then, do we think in terms of these total systems, and how do we establish a high-level sustainable society? That is a problem we have not yet solved. We know how to have a low-level sustainable society, like the Indian village, but I do not think any of us, especially after enjoying a high-level, nonsustainable society, would like it. The unsolved problem of how we develop a high-level sustainable society is not one that public utilities can solve by themselves. On the other hand, the critical question to ask of any institution is whether it is making human survival more or less probable. I would find it hard to assess the public utilities in this regard. They have a lot of pluses; electricity and all that are going to be with us, we hope, for a long time. But, on the other hand, are they going to be adaptable enough, for instance, to push for real energy conservation? Well, Michigan seems to be doing better than anybody, I must say. Detroit Edison has a program for insulating houses, which is extremely enlightened, and one hopes the other utilities will follow this pattern. But it is a hard switch, isn't it, from growth into sustainability, and somehow we have to make this transition.

Whether regulation helps or hinders this process, I do not know. There are times when I think we ought to throw regulation out of the window. We might be better off if we let a few bastards get rich, rather than having the creeping straightjacket of regulation. One of the great problems of society is what I call "antiwork." This is activity which has to be overcome before anything can be done. There is an enormous amount of this, especially in bureaucracies, both public and private. I suspect that the ruin of societies is often due to the uncontrolled growth of antiwork. Governments are especially good at this. This is the real case for Milton Friedman, which is almost the same as the case for anarchism. I love telling Milton he is an anarchist; it really makes him sizzle. I once upset him by pointing out that the market solution to the problem of sex has always been regarded with a mild disfavor. On the other hand, there is a certain virtue in having things rip; let profit-seeking be uncontrolled and then pick up the pieces afterward.

I have been speculating as to whether we could solve the problem of monopoly or market power by unorthodox means. The economic work on market power strikes me as dismal. We have concentrated on developing arbitrary measures of concentration and have neglected the sociology of market power. Who is the bastard? That is the real question of market power; the economics part of it is trivial. If an industry happens to have a bastard, we are all right. He won't play; he'll cut prices and he won't go along with the boys and they won't let him join the country club. The real question is, Who isn't in the country club? All this economic numerology of market power is hardly worth the paper it is written on. You have to look at these things more subtly. I don't know what policy produces bastards, at least in the sociological sense, but there is something in this which I am quite sure we can explore.

I have also been wondering, and I may just be revealing my ignorance here, suppose we abandoned all regulation and simply had a really progressive income tax just to make the rich bastards a little less rich. Suppose we had a decently progressive tax system; couldn't we just forget most quantity and price regulations? We could simply let people get rich and squeeze most of it out of them. We don't have to squeeze it all out of them; most people will do things for little particularly if we maintain the relative structure of incomes, and I suspect we can get all the advantages of the market without its distributional defects if we had a really progressive tax system instead of a fraudulent one as we have now. As you know, the American tax system isn't progressive at all. Over the eight middle percentiles of income it is almost uniform. We could have a much more progressive tax system than we do without really suffering any loss in incentives, and we would end up with a society with a much better morale.

The crucial thing about a society is whether it feels that it means anything; does it feel it's going anywhere? And as the Good Book says, without vision the people perish. This is a profound sociological truth. What sort of vision do we have in our society of the future, that is, of our meaning and significance in the great history of the human race? I have an uneasy feeling that we have lost this, and it is because we have lost this vision that we are floundering around, so we have to have all these silly things around to entertain us like soap operas, Watergate, and all these trivia. But, on the other hand, I think that we can very easily recover a sense of the future, that is, a vision of what we have to do, and that is to create a sustainable society. I think we have about 100 years to do it, maybe

200 years, but not much longer than that. I am quite sure that it can be done if we really put our minds to it and if we catch a vision of it.

2

Can Regulation Curb Corporate Power?

Walter Adams

The subject is how to control corporate power. *Power,* at least as I define it, means insulation from control, immunization from outside disciplinary forces, freedom from external constraints. Corporations, whether they are run by Soviet commissars or by red-blooded American capitalists, have essentially the same motivation—to escape hassling, to lead the quiet life, to sleep peacefully whenever they like, preferably without the assistance of Sominex. And society's interest, on the other hand, is to stop them from doing so—to use the carrot and the stick in such a way as to make them perform society's work and at the lowest possible cost, that is, at the minimum bribe necessary to get the work done.

The genius of capitalism, which highlights the power problem (the problem of distributing economic power in a society), I think, was probably best articulated by Joseph Schumpeter in his landmark work on capitalism.[a] Schumpeter said that the capitalist process is rooted not in classical price competition, but rather in the competition from the new commodity, the new technology, the new source of supply, the new type of organization. This competition commands a decisive cost or quality advantage and strikes not at the margin of profits and outputs of existing firms but at their very foundations and at their very lives. The essence of capitalism, according to Schumpeter, is the perennial gale of creative destruction, in which existing power conditions and entrenched abandon are constantly displaced, by new organizations and by new power complexes. This gale of creative destruction is not only the harbinger of progress, according to Schumpeter, but also the built-in safeguard against the vices of monopoly and privilege.

Now the difficulty with Schumpeter's thesis is that what he conceived of as a control mechanism, working on behalf of society, was of course something business people understood as well as economists. If indeed these gales of creative destruction tend to erode the power position that corporations have in a society, then it is quite natural, and quite understandable, that these corporations would try to devise means for insulating and protecting themselves from the destructive force of those gales. In other words, people in business do not say, "gales of creative destruction, do your thing, blow away, erode our positions of privilege and power."

---

[a]*Capitalism, Socialism, and Democracy,* New York: Harper, 1942.

13

This stance would be masochistic. Instead, quite naturally, they say, "if indeed these gales are blowing, if indeed these gales are effective, we must build storm shelters to protect ourselves from that destructive force." And these storm shelters can be built in two forms: one by private action, that is, you do all those things in a private arena that you can, to insulate yourself from the gale; the other, where private action is either unfeasible or inadequate or ineffective, involves getting the government to build those storm shelters for you.

One favorite storm shelter that corporations have hit upon, of course, is regulation, euphemistically described as "regulation in the public interest." I will cite two of my great heroes in the industrial history of the United States, men who understood this proposition in its pristine purity, who understood it with crystal clarity. The first is Richard Olney, Attorney General in the administration of Grover Cleveland, who had been a director of banks and railroads before he became Attorney General. Once in office he was besieged by former friends in the railroad fraternity to lead a drive for the repeal of the Interstate Commerce Act passed in 1887. Olney came into power in 1892, and the railroads were still bristling under ICC regulation. So they approached their friend Olney to lead a drive aimed at the repeal of the noxious Interstate Commerce Act. But Olney was wiser and cooler than the railroad men. "My impression," he told them, "would be that looking at the matter from a railroad point of view exclusively, it would not be a wise thing to undertake. The Commission, as its functions have now been limited by the courts, is, or can be made, of great use to the railroads. It satisfies the popular clamor for government supervision of the railroads at the same time that that supervision is almost entirely nominal. Further, the older such a Commission gets to be, the more inclined it will be found to take the business and railroad view of things. It thus becomes a sort of barrier between the railroad corporations and the people, and a sort of protection against hasty and crude legislation, hostile to railroad interest. The part of wisdom is not to destroy the Commission, but to utilize it." What genius, what insight, what foresight! In 1892!

My second hero is Judge Elbert H. Gary, President of U.S. Steel. In 1911, you may recall, the Justice Department filed a suit demanding the dissolution of the U.S. Steel Corporation, under the Sherman Act. And a Congressional committee, the famous Stanley Committee, held hearings on what the proper policy of the government ought to be toward such large corporations as U.S. Steel. Elbert H. Gary was a witness before that committee, and he testified as follows:

I realize as fully, I think, as this Committee, that it is very important to consider how the people should be protected against imposition or oppression as a possible result of great aggregations of capital, whether in the possession of corporations or individuals. I believe that is a very important question, and personally I believe that the Sherman Act does not meet and will never fully prevent that. I believe we must come to enforced publicity and government control, even as to prices, and so far as I am concerned, speaking for our company, so far as I have the right, I would be very glad if we had someplace where we could go, to a responsible governmental authority, and say to them, here are our facts and figures, here is our property, here are our costs of production. Now you tell us what we have the right to do and what prices we have the right to charge. I know this is a very extreme view, and I know that the railroads objected to it for a long time, but whether the standpoint of making the most money is concerned, or not, whether it is the wise thing, I believe it is the necessary thing. And it seems to me that corporations have no right to disregard these public questions and these public interests.

Whereupon a member of the committee, Congressman Littleton, then said to him, "your idea then, Sir, is that cooperation is bound to take the place of competition, and that cooperation requires strict governmental supervision." To this Judge Gary replied, "that is a very good statement." So here you have the mighty U.S. Steel Corporation in 1911 asking for government regulation! Now was Judge Gary engaged in a "copout," was he selling out the U.S. Steel Corporation? Not at all. He understood the meaning of power. He understood what was required to insulate corporate power from effective public control. And he seized upon the regulatory mechanism, which he had seen in operation under the aegis of the ICC from 1887 on, as the ideal model.

My reading of history leads me to the conclusion that government regulation is probably the least felicitous experiment in American economic statecraft. I make that statement boldly, realizing that a discussion period is about to follow in which you can register your deep-seated dissent. Let me try to support that proposition. I think, first, that regulatory commissions tend to develop an undue identification with the industries they are supposed to regulate. More often than not, they seem to protect the regulated industries from competition, rather than the public from exploitation. Indeed, it is not too extreme to suggest, as our experience (especially with the ICC) indicates, that what starts out as regulation ends up as protection. The power to license becomes the power to exclude; the regulation of rates, a system of price supports; the surveillance of mergers, an instrument of concentration; the supervision of business practices, a pretext for harassing the weak, the unorganized, and the politically impotent; and the assurance of a needed public service, an excuse for public subsidies and bailouts. Once an industry becomes the government's chosen instrument for effectuating a public purpose, regulation becomes, as Henry Simons saw long ago, "an apology for governmental enforcement of minimum prices and wages at levels higher than monopolies could maintain without the support of law." Regulation becomes the means of officially sanctioning and legitimitizing the chosen instrument's performance, no matter how deplorable such performance may be—whether the monopolist is Penn Central, Lockheed, Consolidated Edison, or, going back some years, the East India Company. There is nothing new under the sun! You read Adam Smith on the East India Company, and you can substitute Lockheed and understand what is going on. It's the same kind of phenomenon. Once you are wedded to that kind of regulatory scheme, the public is stuck with its chosen instrument.

The public has only two broad alternatives. It can refuse to take the permissiveness route of coddling the chosen instrument which is guilty of economic misfeasance, malfeasance, and nonfeasance. The public can insist on administering strong and distasteful medicine in the hope of curing the patient or, if that fails, to let the patient die. The other alternative, and this seems to be the one we consistently elect to embrace, is to maintain the patient—in whatever state of disrepair and irrespective of the continuing deterioration—simply because "the patient is all we've got." We don't restore the patient to health; we just keep him or her alive and postpone the evil day to some time in the future.

The second difficulty with regulation is that, at best, it is a negative force for right conduct. A regulatory commission can refuse to approve a price increase, but it cannot compel its regulatees to lower production costs. And I think that's of capital importance, that's "where it's at," you see. The commission cannot compel the scrapping of old plants or the construction of new ones. It cannot force additional expenditures on research and development or command greater progressiveness in innovation and in invention. It cannot penalize management for its incompetence, for its lack of imagination, or for its lack of creativity because it does not have a clear view of what potentially attainable cost reductions are. It has no way, therefore, of stopping the great vice of monopoly, namely, the monopolist's tendency to lead the quiet life and to squander society's treasure in the form of excessive cost. Limiting the monopolist to a fair return may be the essence of the regulatory process, but it does not achieve society's central objective. Put differently, regulation is often a pass-through mechanism for the inefficiency, cost escalation, and lethargy of pampered managements luxuriating in an ambience of governmental permissiveness.

Third, regulation, whatever its short-run, static virtues, is not a substitute for but a complement to competition. That is, it cannot function effectively without some exogenous force to discipline the conservative bias of both regulatees and regulators. Experience shows, especially in transportation, but also in communications, that even peripheral competition plays a more significant role than straight regulation in forcing innovations on bureaucratic managers and their overly permissive guardians. I will not go into, I will simply cite and invite your attention to, the role of TVA, the role of the nonscheduled airlines, the role of international charters and excursions in transatlantic travel, the role of the haulers of agricultural commodities in the trucking industry. It is these marginal competitors, operating at the periphery and in the interstices of a regulated industry, who have done so much to demonstrate what innovations are possible, practical, and profitable, and who, more often than not, have suffered regulatory euthanasia for performing that invaluable public service. You know, I cannot help but wonder if the automobile industry had been a regulated industry at the outset, whether a "madman" like Henry Ford would have ever been allowed to implement his price policy which, as you know, contravened the conventional wisdom of the then prevailing orthodoxy. I doubt whether any regulatory commission would have approved his notions of pricing.

What, then, is the solution? Obviously, at least as far as I'm concerned, I think that deregulation, wherever possible, is the answer. That is, in industries which are naturally competitive industries, there really is no excuse for the government's playing a role, because the government will only be a protective device for vested interest. It will be a mask for privilege, a shield for monopoly. It will not be an agency for the public interest. An outstanding and admittedly extreme example of this proposition is the trucking industry. Here you have an industry which is naturally competitive; there are no great economies of scale; entry is easy. The only reason the trucking industry was ever brought under regulation of the ICC through the Motor Carrier Act of 1935 was the insistence of the railroads. The railroads argued that the trucking industry was affording it "excessive, destructive," (and you can add euphemistic adjectives according to taste) competition. And, how do you eliminate that competition?—by bringing it under ICC control. And the ICC has become an instrument for excluding the entry of newcomers, protecting the grandfather carriers, promoting concentration, and encouraging mergers. And, if you look at the rate orders, to my knowledge, the ICC has never in its history since 1935 issued a maximum rate order in the trucking industry. It was always a minimum rate order. Now that tells us something as to the purpose of that type of regulation. Indeed, given the competitive pattern, I would argue that the entire surface transportation industry can now be safely deregulated and subjected to the discipline of the competitive market with such surveillance as the antitrust laws provide. The ICC can safely retire from the scene.

But this is an extreme case. There are other industries now regulated which obviously do not fit the deregulation model. And then the great question becomes, which is always the question of the law, where do you draw the line; that is, how do you accommodate a conflict in policy, a conflict between the dictates of regulation and the dictates of competition? And by the way, I should make it clear that to me competition does not mean keeping prices low and making sure that corporations do not overcharge the consumer by 2 cents per pound of meat or 1 penny per ton-mile carried, and so on. That really isn't the name of the game. What concerns me is the distribution of power in a society. To me, competition means decentralization of power. It is the economic approximation of my political ideal which is summarized in the Federalist Papers, and I find no greater work that I have ever seen on the nature of power and the control of power than the Federalist Papers. I think the issue of where to draw the line was very clearly articulated by two brilliant judges on the U.S. Supreme Court in the famous case of *McLean Trucking Company v. the United States*. Both judges were liberals. Speaking for the majority was Justice Ruteledge. And the question was, in that case, whether the merger of several companies into Associated Transport was to be approved, and whether the ICC had final jurisdiction in this matter. And Justice Ruteledge said "yes." Here was some of his reasoning: "Congress however neither made the antitrust laws wholly inapplicable to the transportation industry, nor has it authorized the Commission in passing on a proposed merger to ignore their policy. Congress recognized that the process of consolidating motor carriers would result in some diminuation of competition and might result in the creation of monopoly. To prevent the latter effect and to make certain that the former was permitted only where appropriate, to further the national transportation policy, it placed in the Commission power to control such developments." Then, skipping a little bit, he continues: "Hence the fact that carriers participating in the properly authorized consolidation, may obtain immunity from prosecution under the antitrust laws, in no sense relieves the Commission from its duty, as an administrative matter, to consider the effect of the merger on competitors and on the general competitive conditions in the industry."

The dissent, by Justice Douglas, agreed. But there was a difference in emphasis. "I would read paragraph five of the Transportation Act so as to make for the greatest possible accommodation between the principles of competition and the national transportation policy. The occasions for the exercise of the administrative authority to grant exemptions from the antitrust laws should be closely confined to those where the transportation need is clear." In other words, you let competition have its way except where the objectives of serving the public interest cannot be achieved by any other means. In other words, you make competition the paramount standard in judging the public interest. And you try to withhold the regulatory hand as much as you possibly can. You look at a "natural monopoly," and you, as a regulator, inquire to what extent is it a natural monopoly, to what extent is it an unnatural monopoly, and to what extent can we serve the public interest by diminishing the monopolistic component in this "natural" monopoly. You can look upon the regulatory commission, then, not as a professional nay-sayer who says to the regulatee, "no you can't do that." But instead you can look upon the regulatory process as a creative process, where the commission is an umpire stimulating and structuring competition to the maximum extent feasible within the constraints of technology to achieve the public purpose. The rule should be minimum grants of power necessary to effect the regulatory goal.

Let me try to translate that into some specifics—first, on the front of intermode competition. Again let's take technology as the outside, limiting constraint. There is no need to permit any erosion of intermode competition by letting railroads go into trucking, water carriage, and competing modes of transportation. If you take the communications field, broadcasting, it's okay to have somebody own an AM radio station. Obviously you can't have two corporations operating over the same frequency. But query, does the owner of the AM station in Kalamazoo also have to be the operator of the FM station? Does she or he also have to be the operator of the TV station? As the operator of the VHF station, does she or he also have to control the UHF station? If she or he controls all these, does that control have to include possibly the only newspaper in that town? My answer to you is "no." And if there is one owner of all these facilities in a town, the question is, what about multiple ownership across the country? There is nothing in technology that militates toward the concentration of that kind of power. That is a manmade decision, the manner in which the regulatory commission chooses to structure the market. It is not the will of God; it is not a law of nature; there is no technological imperative that militates toward the kind of concentration of power that we find in the broadcasting and media industry.

Second, with respect to vertical integration of telephones, I question the amount of vertical integration that is necessary in the telephone business on technological grounds. For example, I read the decision in the case of *ITT v. General Telephone and Electric,* where General Telephone and Electric was forced to divest itself of some of its equipment suppliers if it was to acquire Hawaiian Telephone. And if that kind of decision comes down with respect to General Telephone and Electric, I must confess that I cannot understand why we continue to tolerate the vertical integration between ATT and Western Electric. This, of course, brings up the whole question of interconnection and whether a regulated company should be in what is essentially a conflict-of-interest position, because of the absence of arm's-length buying—a conflict between relying on its own captive suppliers and affording outside companies, outside equipment manufacturers, to compete effectively for its business.

The third issue is the conglomerate holding company. You look at a monstrosity like Penn Central, and you find that Penn Central was not just a railroad. Penn Central operated the New York Knickerbockers, the Keystone Pipeline, and Executive Jet Aviation. Maybe if they had stuck to the railroad business and the railroad business exclusively, they might have done a better job. I also invite your attention to the fact that, of course, these conglomerate operations are not subject to regulation. This is a means of avoiding or circumventing regulation. And if you look at the holding company device which is coming into increasing use in this field, where you have a regulated carrier over here and then a vast conglomerate empire out there, that empire is beyond control. It reminds you of Will Rogers' definition of a holding company: "A holding company is something where you hand an accomplice the goods, while the policeman searches you." That's the kind of regulatory control that is currently exercised over holding company empires in "regulated" industries.

To come back to where I started, if we view the power problem in Schumpeter's terms, and if we understand what the motivation of entrepreneurs is, then we also understand what the strategy of society has to be. This is not a question of entrepreneurs being rapacious exploiters trying to shortchange the public. Nothing of the sort. The problem is built into the structure within which these people have to operate. And the same applies to the regulatory commission. When people say to me today that the solution for the oil industry is government regulation, I must say that I cringe. I cringe only slightly less than when I hear people suggest that the oil industry be nationalized. I grieve for those simplistic souls who would nationalize the oil industry and combine economic and political power in the same friendly hands that brought us Vietnam and Watergate. I am a conservative radical. I am a conservative because I read the Federalist Papers and I take them literally. I am a radical because I believe in decentralization of power, both economic and political, because I think that that is the only kind of societal structure compatible with individual liberty.

3

Recent Developments in the Natural Gas Industry—A New Perspective

David S. Schwartz

Introduction

A close observer of the natural gas industry would be correct in describing the changes that have taken place in the last few years as kaleidoscopic in nature and unique in their characteristics. This is true not only because of the variety of new problems that have beset the industry, but also because of the complexity of public policy issues currently challenging regulatory commissions. The traditionalists who have worked with the questions of accounting regulation, the determination of an appropriate cost of service, rate base, and the general question of legitimizing revenue requirements will find that today's problems are distinctly different, requiring a new focus in assessing policy formulation.

The analysis that follows[a] will illustrate the basic changes that have occurred in regulatory policies and procedures that reflect a marked shift in operational and financial risks from investors to consumers with significant attendant costs to consumers. This additional burden on ratepayers in a period of general inflation is questionable on equity grounds and, in many instances, poses many unresolved questions of social policy. Last, the use of the gas shortage as a justification for institutionalizing inequitable and economically unsound proposals causes serious problems to surface for those concerned with fair and "evenhanded" regulation.

The objective of this chapter is to delineate the specific areas concerning the public policy issues currently relating to the natural gas pipeline and producer industry. To the extent that decisions in these industry sectors affect the distribution companies, the special problems associated with this interplay, particularly as it relates to market structure implications, will also be explored.

Recent Pipeline Rate Filings

For the traditionalist, the following information will indicate some of the familiar aspects of current proceedings before the Federal Power Commission. Of course, there are a large number of rate-increase proposals cur-

---

[a]The views and opinions expressed in this statement are entirely personal and are submitted in an individual capacity. They do not necessarily reflect the views of the Federal Power Commission.

21

rently on file with the Commission; as of the end of 1973, pending pipeline rate suspensions totalled more than $1 billion annually. A recent proposal, filed April 15, 1974, in which United Gas Pipe Line Company (Docket No. RP74-83) requested an annual rate increase of $82.9 million illustrates the general order of magnitude of the rate of return requested. United filed for a return of 10.4 percent overall and with a capitalization of approximately 58 percent of long-term debt, 22 percent of preferred stock, and 20 percent of common equity. This is estimated to produce a return of 16.99 percent on common equity.

A recent settlement approved by the Federal Power Commission on April 5, 1974, concerning Transcontinental Gas Pipe Line Corporation (Docket No. RP73-69), is indicative of the type of return currently permitted by the Commission on a 14.38 percent on common equity. Last, the approval of a settlement on February 14, 1974, proposed by El Paso Natural Gas Company (Docket No. RP69-6, *et al.*), covering six separate rate filings collected over a 3 1/2 year period from March 1969 to November 1973, raises two problems which will be explored subsequently. First, the objective of adopting a purchased gas adjustment clause to prevent "pancake" filings appears to have been illusory. Second, the unique proposal in which the customers of El Paso in a settlement agreement providing for refunds of over $50 million agreed to forego $31.5 million in order to permit the creation of an exploration reserve poses the question of the advisability and equity of an involuntary contribution of consumer-contributed capital.

Purchased Gas Adjustment Clauses

In extraordinary action, for the first time, the Federal Power Commission amended its regulations to permit the inclusion of purchased gas adjustment provisions in pipeline company tariffs.[1] The importance of this determination should be seen in light of the fact that for the great majority of natural gas pipeline companies, the single largest element in the cost of service is the cost of purchased gas.

To minimize the adverse financial effects on the pipeline resulting from escalating purchased gas costs (producer well-head price increases), the Commission allows the pipeline companies to modify their rates, with proper notice, when the change is at least 1 mill per Mcf (million cubic feet) of annual jurisdictional sales. The Commission concluded that it was desirable to curb the frequency of general rate increase filings because of the administrative delays involved in final rate determination.

These rate changes are permitted above the rates established after the submission of a cost study based on actual costs for the most recent available 12-month period. Pipeline rate increases to reflect the increase in the cost of purchased gas from producers from this base period are permitted on a semiannual basis.

Legitimate concerns of adopting the purchased gas adjustment clauses were raised by two major parties: the Tennessee Valley Municipal Gas Association and the American Public Gas Association. Their objections were twofold: to isolating one element in the cost of service, and to abandoning a long-established approach in which possible cost increases may be offset either by other reduced costs or by increasing revenues. They contended that the pipeline is obligated to file for rate increases and present a full cost of service which permitted the matching of costs and revenues. They charged that Order No. 452 violated the basic matching concept of the Natural Gas Act.

They further pointed out that the 3-year period provided in the Order before the Commission reviews the impact of automatic purchased gas adjustments to rates may permit a company to collect excessive rates for a long period of time, and they contended that the filing of a cost study after 36 months is inadequate for effective consumer protection. Last, they insisted that a PGA (purchased gas adjustment) clause would remove a strong incentive on the part of the pipeline to bargain vigorously with its supplier for lower rates.

The initiation of the PGA program by the Commission should be viewed as the first step to insulate pipelines from spiraling costs and to provide an immediate passing on of higher charges to consumers. In the 1960s when pipelines were in an excess earnings position, there was no automatic downward rate adjustment; and the only means of obtaining rate reductions, other than negotiated rate settlement, was through a lengthy process of staff investigation, hearing, and ultimate Commission decision in which the new rate levels would be established prospectively. It would appear that the *quid pro quo* would dictate that no upward automatic rate adjustments in this current period should be sanctioned.

Incremental Pricing

Another significant problem influencing the level as well as the impact of pipeline rate increases is the current unavailability of adequate conventional wellhead sources of natural gas and the decision to obtain supplemental supplies. The importation of liquefied natural gas (LNG) and current synthetic natural gas (SNG) and coal gasification proposals have raised many questions as to the appropriate pricing procedures for these high-cost supplies. In addition, there are a number of related considerations concerning Commission jurisdiction, the interrelationship with the curtailment program, as well as the issue of rate design.

With supplemental supplies ranging as high as $2.99 per Mcf, but generally in the range of $1.40 to $1.60 per Mcf, the traditional pipeline pricing practice of "rolled-in" costs of gas supplies has been rejected by the Commission. In contrast to the prices of these supplemental sources, the wellhead prices for conventional supplies are indicated by the most recent Commission nationwide area rate for new gas set at $.42 per Mcf exclusive of production taxes,[2] the highest optional price allowed of $.55, and the highest price under limited short-term sales of $.50.

In a landmark opinion, involving Columbia LNG Corporation,[3] the Commission determined that the importation of LNG from Algeria should be sold on an incremental basis. They concluded that rolled-in prices would meet neither the economic efficiency nor the equity standard. First, they found that those customers that do not recieve any benefit from LNG should not be burdened with the cost of this supply and, second, that a market test should be required for an efficient allocation of resources.

In the original opinion, the Commission prohibited the pipeline from selling LNG to a distributor customer which did not have a separate incremental rate schedule for resale purposes. This requirement was subsequently eliminated, and the Commission retained only the requirement of incremental pricing at the pipeline level. While the U.S. Court of Appeals for the Fifth Circuit remanded this case to the Commission because the hearing record did not provide substantial evidence to support the adoption of incremental pricing, it is anticipated that the incremental procedure will ultimately prevail.

The pipeline companies and the distributors opposed the use of an incremental pricing approach in this case for varying reasons. The pipeline companies contended that it would result in undermining the project because they could not obtain financing given the uncertainties associated with finding customers to accept the higher-priced supply. In addition, they contended that it is impossible to earmark the LNG supply for separate rate tratment and that to attempt to do so would provide tremendous administrative difficulties. Last, they argued that all customers should bear the costs equally of all sources of gas on a rolled-in basis. The distribution companies contended that the Commission was invading the jurisdiction of the state commissions and that the effort to prohibit sales unless the distributor has an incremental tariff is illegal.

From an economic standpoint, in order for the correct price signals to be effective for resource allocation, it is essential that incremental pricing be implemented at all levels so that the final user will be faced with the real cost of alternative fuels. In addition, as will be discussed later, in this period of curtailments, obviously, it is the lower-priority customers who will require these high-cost supplemental supplies, and the general ratepayer should not subsidize the industrial users who have alternative choices to supply their fuel requirements. Undoubtedly, as a marketing strategy, when incremental costs are higher than average cost, rolled-in prices will benefit the firm in maximizing their profit opportunities in competition with other fuel suppliers. Nonetheless, in this instance, the use of average cost pricing results in residential users subsidizing industrial users as well as resource waste and inefficiency.

Pipeline Rate Design—A Major Modification of Seaboard

Another manifestation of the upheaval caused by current gas shortages is the recent opinion in a United Gas Pipe Line Company case which drastically modified the Atlantic Seaboard method of cost classification.[4] In this proceeding Federal Power Commission staff argued that the rationale for the Seaboard formula assumed a close relationship between installed pipeline capacity and peak-day sales, and they contended that in light of the present inadequate supplies and increased curtailments on United's system, the two-part rate was no longer justified.

The Commission concluded, as a matter of judgment, that 75 percent of fixed costs should be assigned to the commodity rate and 25 percent to the demand charge. The Commission, while favorably disposed to the merits of the staff proposal of a one-part rate, concluded that the sudden abrupt change could be "disruptive to United's system and at this time a more moderate shift would be in the public interest."

The Commission's desire to modify the Seaboard allocation method and assign more costs to the commodity charge was signaled in an earlier El Paso opinion.[5] While the Commission rejected a proposal to switch from a modified Seaboard method and retained the unmodified Seaboard approach, they indicated that they would "carry out a searching reappraisal of the question of cost classification and allocation in the light of the present increasing needs for gas and the current shortage as well as an overall review of rate design." While the record did not permit any reverse "tilting" of the Seaboard rate in this instance, the thinking of the Commission is reflected in the above-mentioned United case.

The obvious effect of shifting a higher proportion of costs to the commodity component in the rate design is to provide economic pressure for industrial users with multipurpose plant to shift to other fuels. The implied objectives are to conserve gas for residential and small commercial uses and to discourage the use of gas for the larger-volume industrial and boiler fuel purposes. If the cost of alternative fuels to industrial users, who are indifferent as to which fuel they use, is lower than or equal to the cost of gas, then this approach will constrain gas consumption. Unfortunately, the cost of other fuels has risen drastically and is greater proportionally than natural gas, in the last few years, and the use of price as a constraint on the industrial demand for gas, in most cases, has not been successful. The only alternative available to fulfill the objectives of conserving gas for higher-priority uses in a supply deficiency period, therefore, is to promulgate carefully structured curtailment procedures.

Additional Rate Design Proposals

In proceedings currently before the Commission, two pipelines—United Gas Pipe Line Company (Docket No. RP74-21) and Consolidated Gas Supply Corporation (Docket No. RP74-32)—are proposing radical changes in rate design to recover fixed costs in this period of declining sales due to the unavailability of natural gas. Specifically, United proposes to incorporate in its tariff a Volume Variation Adjustment Clause (VVAC) which would allow "cost-volume" adjustments in commodity rates every 6 months if currently estimated sales differed from annual sales used in the pipeline's last cost of service.

In effect, the pipeline proposes to increase the commodity rate if the volume of gas available for sale in the future is less than the projected sales volumes, and to reflect the increase in revenue requirement in the commodity charge. In support of its position, United contends that the test-year approach used to determine cost of service and the commodity rate determination based on annual sales volumes are inadequate in a time of declining sales volumes, and that the fixed costs must be recovered through increases in the commodity charge.

The staff witness opposed United's automatic commodity rate adjustments on the following bases:

1. The United proposal would result in an automatic reassignment of nonjurisdictional costs to jurisdictional customers.
2. Rates would be revised without any considerations of potential cost offsets.
3. There was an unwarranted shift of risk from the owners of the pipeline to its customers with potential adverse effects on management incentives.[6]

In a recent rate increase application filed July 16, 1974, Transcontinental Gas Pipe Line Corporation (Docket No. 75-3) requested $48.6 million annually over and above the $51.3 million filed for in December 1973 (Docket No. 74-48). In the latest filing Transcontinental included a volumetric variation adjustment clause to reflect the impact of declining supplies. In this connection, the company attributes almost 70 percent of the proposed increase to a decline of over 184 billion cubic feet in supply since its earlier rate filing.

These are good examples of the manner in which pipeline companies propose to insulate themselves from the operational and business risks associated with the uncertainties of adequate new supplies of gas to assure full utilization of capacity. While there is some merit in the contention that the Commission should adopt policies to keep the company "whole," this does not address the critical question whether the VVAC is the appropriate mechanism. The earlier discussion indicated that consumers had no automatic protection in the 1960s when rates and earnings were excessive and when downward adjustments were uncertain and time-consuming. Undoubtedly, the traditional rate hearing and settlement procedures have the same advantages currently as they did in the past.

Curtailment Priorities

On January 8, 1973, the Commission issued a statement of policy establishing eight priority classifications to be applied by jurisdictional pipelines when curtailment of contractual demands was necessary.[7] Subsequently, the Commission added a ninth category of interruptible industrial user which, in effect, is the lowest priority. An examination of these categories indicates a stratification from the highest priority classification of residential and small commercial to the lowest interruptible large-requirement industrial customer.

In time, the Commission issued further orders amending Order No. 467 so as to require the inclusion of tariff provisions, affording sufficient flexibility for pipelines to respond to emergency situations during periods of curtailment when supplemental deliveries are required to prevent irreparable injury to life or property. As one would expect, there have been many requests for interim relief and special exception to the Commission's curtailment procedures.

The Commission has been steadfast in implementing its priority classifications, and while granting emergency relief, they have required supportive data and have ordered hearings to ultimately determine the disposition of any variance from its general policy. In Order No. 467-C, the Commission stressed that the conditions that attach to the granting of interim relief from curtailment, pending final action after hearing, would require a pay-back obligation if special relief was denied, and that the period over which the granted relief would be extended was to be determined on the basis of the individual facts in each instance.

The Fifth Circuit Court of Appeals affirmed the FPC decision to grant Texas Gulf Sulphur Co. only partial relief and ordered repayment of past overtakes.[8] The Commission had initially granted Texas Gulf additional volumes of gas under interim "extraordinary relief" with respect to curtailments by United Gas Pipe Line Company (Docket Nos. RP71-29 and RP71-120). Subsequently, the Commission determined that Texas Gulf failed to demonstrate that it could not use other fuels for general purposes together with the allotment of gas under the curtailment program to prevent irreparable injury to its sulfur mine.

A recent FPC staff Gas Curtailment Report indicates that in contrast to the actual curtailment in the April 1973-March 1974 period of approximately 7 percent [1.2 trillion cubic feet (Tcf)], the projected deficiency in the April 1974-March 1975 period will increase to 9 percent (1.8 Tcf). What appears to be a relatively modest 7 percent curtailment experienced in 1973-1974, in fact, masks the serious curtailments of a number of major pipelines, such as 32.3 percent of United Gas Pipe Line Company and 29.3 percent of Arkansas-Louisiana Gas Company in contrast to minor curtailments of about 1 percent for Transwestern Pipeline Company and Northern Natural Gas Co.[9]

Low-priority industrial users have appealed to gas distributors and pipeline companies to assist in mitigating the impact of their interruptions. For example, the Columbia Gas Transmission Corp., with the support of the Public Service Commission of Maryland and Baltimore Gas and Electric Company, is currently protesting the Commission's priority classifications and proposing pro rata reductions rather than curtailments based upon Commission priorities. The Public Service Commission of Maryland made it clear that there are serious implications with respect to curtailing low-priority industrial users in the state such as Bethlehem Steel, Kennecott Refining Corporation, Black and Decker Manufacturing Co., and a chemical subsidiary, W.R. Grace Co., which would seriously affect employment and plant operation. Of course, the objections raised in microcosm illustrate the broader economic implications of a curtailment program which ranks industrial usage at the lower levels. It is apparent that if curtailments became more severe and affected a larger number of pipeline systems, without significant additions of new gas supplies, serious problems of industrial output, employment, and price inflation are in the offing.

Supplemental Sources of Supply

Because of the current unavailability of natural gas, there has been a proliferation of projects involving imported liquefied natural gas (LNG), synthetic natural gas (SNG), and coal gas. The initial importation of LNG, discussed earlier, was certificated under a filing by El Paso Algeria, which was held to be a jurisdictional company under the Natural Gas Act.[10] The authorized volumes for base load purposes was 1 billion cubic feet (Bcf) of gas per day. This was the first large-scale base load importation of Algerian

LNG, which previously had been brought into the country in smaller shipments for peaking purposes.

The import price for Columbia LNG and Consolidated LNG at Cove Point, Maryland was $.77 per million Btu; for Southern Energy at Savannah, Georgia, the initial price was $.83 per million Btu. In contrast, the recent filing by Trunkline LNG Company (CP74-138, et al.) to import 420 Mcf of gas per day from Algeria to be delivered near Lake Charles, Louisiana, reflects a cost of service in the first year estimated at $1.61 per Mcf. Last, it is interesting to note that another potential area for LNG is Indonesia. Pacific Indonesia LNG Co., a newly formed subsidiary of Pacific Lighting Corp., recently applied for authority (CP74-160, application filed November 30, 1973) to import from Indonesia 554 Mcf per day over a 20-year period at an initial price of $1.58 per million Btu. In contrast to the Commission's holding with respect to LNG imports, they disclaimed jurisdiction with regard to the construction of synthetic gas processing plants in a case involving Algonquin SNG Corp. (CP73-35).[11] The Commission concluded that the naphtha-fed gas reforming plant was not subject to its jurisdiction and that synthetic gas when unmixed with natural gas is "artificial" gas exempt from regulation under the Natural Gas Act. They made clear that jurisdiction attaches to synthetic gas once it becomes mixed with natural gas flowing in interstate commerce. Subsequent decisions involving numerous SNG reforming plants were decided to be outside FPC jurisdiction.

The future availability of supplemental sources of gas remains uncertain because many SNG proposals have been beset with difficulties due to unavailable feedstock or the prohibitive cost of feedstock. For example, the original Algonquin SNG proposal in which the Commission authorized the SNG sales to Algonquin Gas Transmission of up to 120,000 Mcf per day at a rate of $1.80 per Mcf in November 1972, has recently been refiled, and an offer of settlment was approved by the FPC on March 14, 1974 at a rate of $2.99 per Mcf.

Similar increases are reflected in the filing by Natural Gas Pipeline Company of America (CP74-81) which will purchase approximately 67,000 million Btu (MMBtu) per day of synthetic gas from Phillips Petroleum. In September 1973, Natural's application reflected a price of $1.66/MMBtu. Currently, the contract with Phillips calls for deliveries in 1976 at $2.80/MMBtu.

The current unavailability of feedstock, usually naphtha, but ranging from ethane through naphtha, has caused a number of SNG projects to be abandoned. For example, the Tecon Gasification Project of Texas Eastern Transmission Corporation, which proposed construction of a liquid hydrocarbon gasification plant in Louisiana, was recently abandoned because of inadequate feedstock supply. Originally, the project was to have produced

400,000 Mcf per day of pipeline-quality gas from foreign and domestic naphtha at $1.26 per Mcf, when it was filed in November 1972 (CP72-100). Additional SNG projects that had been withdrawn include Cities Service Gas Company (CP73-301), involving 125,000 Mcf of synthetic gas per day, Trunkline Gas (CP73-58), Columbia Gas Transmission (CP73-342 and CP74-100), and Transcontinental Gas Pipe Line Corp. (CP73-21) for a reforming plant near Chester, Pennsylvania, because of the failure to reach agreement with the National Iranian Gas Co. with respect to feedstock.

The first two coal gasification projects to come before the Commission involve El Paso Natural Gas and a jointly sponsored project by Transwestern Pipeline Company and Pacific Lighting Corporation. In a separate proceeding involving these companies, as it did in the Algonquin SNG case, the Commission refused to assert jurisdiction until the synthetic gas produced from the gasification facilities was mixed with natural gas.[12] The same distinction of "artificial" gas was used to disclaim any regulatory jurisdiction over coal gasification facilities.

The El Paso project (Docket No. CP73-131), consisting of two wholly owned subsidiaries, one for mining operations and the other to construct and operate the coal gasification plant, proposes the production of 280,000 Mcf per day of synthetic gas at an estimated cost of $1.51 per Mcf in the first full year of operation. The Transwestern-Pacific Lighting project (Docket No. CP73-211), involving separate companies for mining and coal gasification, is estimated to produce 250,000 Mcf per day at a cost of $1.32 per Mcf in the first year of operation.

In the El Paso proceeding, the staff witness raised a number of fundamental questions which he considered crucial before the approval of the project could be recommended.[13] He raised the fundamental question whether potential available supplies of natural gas from conventional wellhead sources and whether current prospective Commission policies would permit El Paso to augment its required gas supply in the future without the need for higher-cost coal gas. Second, he indicated that the market price of substitutable energy, including intrastate prices for natural gas, was approximately one-half the cost of the proposed price for coal gas. He pointed out additional problems concerning the operational uncertainties with respect to the coal gasification project, and the shifting of risks from the company and its investors to the customers. Last, he recommended incremental pricing based on equity as well as on resource criteria.

With regard to the latter point, he suggested a modification of the Commission's incremental method adopted in the Columbia decision (Opinion No. 622-A) in which the gas would be offered to the highest priority customers, subject to curtailment before lower-priority customers could contract for the gas. In addition, his proposal would permit changes over time, and when subsequent customers with higher priority are curtailed, they could displace those customers currently receiving gas under the incremental tariff. In effect, this would symmetrically relate the Commission's curtailment procedures with the incremental pricing objectives of high-cost supplies.

On June 13, 1974, an administrative law judge recommended approval of the $447 million Transwestern-Pacific Lighting coal gasification proposal. He rejected the applicants' position that the failure to allow an open-ended cost of service would prevent financing and required that an initial rate per Mcf be submitted for FPC approval. The new rate is to be filed 6 months before the expected start-up date, together with an explanatory statement and final financing plans. The law judge approved a return of 15 percent on common equity and determined that the unit cost estimated at $1.32 per Mcf would increase to $1.60 to $1.70 per Mcf between the present period and 1978 (anticipated date of coal gas production) because of inflation. Last, he would require a reduction of the filed price in the event SNG production falls below 50 percent of the projected level of 250,000 Mcf per day for a period longer than 30 consecutive days by the *amount of common equity return* reflected in the rates.

One week later (June 21, 1974), another administrative law judge issued an initial decision conditionally approving the El Paso $460 million coal gasification project. He accepted the 15 percent rate of return on equity and the "rolled-in" cost of synthetic gas supply proposed by the pipeline company. He rejected the automatic passing on of purchased gas for the initial production cost of the coal gas. Last, his decision provided for the elimination of the return to equity capital if the load factor falls below 25 percent.

It is clear from both of these initial decisions that the customer's share of risk of these projects is far greater than that of the business enterprise. While the equity investors cannot be assured of a return *on* their investment, they can be assured of a return *of* their investment. Since 75 percent of the capital for both projects will be obtained from debt sources, the senior capital is well protected and the burden on consumers to meet interest cost is established. If risk-taking of this magnitude is shifted to consumers, one can legitimately ask whether they should not share in the benefits if the project is successful, to a greater extent than the privilege of paying higher prices for coal gas. As a justification for the consumers assuming the major burden of the operational and financial risks, both decisions point to the need for supplemental supplies in this period of gas shortage and the uncertainty and expense of other alternative sources of gas. It is appropriate to ask whether in these instances the gas shortage provides the rationale to transfer the major share of the risks to consumers and whether these projects would stand the economic test of an unprotected market.

Last, the crucial question concerning LNG, SNG, or coal gas is whether the substantial potential natural gas reserves that remain to be developed make these high-cost supplies uneconomic, inadvisable, and unnecessary. The question of appropriate public policy to develop these potential reserves will be considered in the context of producer regulation and market structure in the subsequent discussion.

The Advance Payments Program

At the end of last year, the Commission extended its advance payments program for another 2 years, that is, through December 1975.[14] For the first time, advances made to producers in Alaska were included. This advance payment program was initiated in October, 1970, and has been renewed on an annual basis subject to the evaluation of the effectiveness of advance payments in eliciting interstate gas supplies. In the most recent renewal, the Commission concluded that the program "has continued to make its objectives of bringing additional gas supplies into the interstate market at an acceptable cost to the nation's gas consumers."

The information currently available indicates that advance payment commitments made through July 30, 1973 by 26 major interstate pipelines since the inception of the program totaled $1.93 billion. Of this amount, $1.26 billion was actually advanced. The pipelines reported the advance as pertaining to estimated total proved reserves of 26.8 Tcf (trillion cubic feet) (10.3 Tcf in the lower 48 states) and estimated probable reserves of 15.6 Tcf (including 9.6 Tcf in the lower 48 states).

In its latest order, the Commission affirmed its approval of rate base treatment for advances, which results in the acquisition of a working interest by a pipeline affiliate, and the Commission extended this approval to cover advances resulting in a working interest for a pipeline as well. The producer sector objected to the pipeline company's providing advances to its own affiliate or for its own exploration and development program on the basis that it would favor the use of their own funds in contrast to making their funds available to independent producers.

Finally, it is interesting to note that in a recent decision, [15] the Commission denied a proposal by Michigan Wisconsin Pipe Line Company (Docket No. RP71-112) to include a $5 million advance payment to a Canadian company in its rate base. It determined that the uncertainties of current Canadian export policies appear to make it "little more than speculative that the gas involved would ever be received by United States customers."

The New York Commission and the American Public Gas Association have consistently opposed the advance payment program. They contend that the consumer should not have to pay the return associated with the advances being part of the pipeline company's rate base. In effect, they contend that the producer or pipeline affiliate should raise capital to support exploration and development of gas supplies and that this is a form of hidden price increase to consumers. They further contend that producer rates should be determined with a direct and explicit indication of incentives for supply elicitation.

The New York Commission had recommended termination of the capitalization of advance payments, contending there was no evidence that advance payments have been instrumental in inducing producers to bid for and develop offshore leases. The Commission's response was to indicate that the primary purpose of the advance payment was to aid in capital formation so as to *accelerate* the addition of new gas supplies to the interstate market. The Commission said:

We do not now state, nor have we stated, that the 9.5 Tcf of proven reserves would never have been found or developed absent the advance payment program. However, analysis of the data and comments filed herein indicates that this program was a ''significant and necessary factor in speeding the capital formation which led to the exploration, development and dedication of 9.5 Tcf of proven reserves from onshore as well as offshore for use by the interstate market at the time in which it occurred.''

In a calculation incorporated in Order No. 465 (issued December 29, 1972), the Commission estimated that the added cost to consumers for the 8.7 Tcf of proven reserves was about $.025 per Mcf. The additional revenues paid by consumers through advance payments appears to be $217.5 million.

The advance payment program is a middle ground between the direct contribution of consumer capital—for example, in the form of a surcharge—and the more traditional assumption of risk by the business enterprise. While there are many fundamental questions of equity and the determination of appropriate consumer costs, it is difficult to logically relate the involuntary contribution of consumer capital to the basic doctrine of the ''free enterprise system'' in the classic conceptual sense. This is one area where the judgmental aspects of decisionmaking should reflect basic principles in policy formulation.

The Use of a Surcharge on Consumer Rates to Fund Exploration and Development Programs

A new and novel proposal to use a surcharge on top of established gas rates is currently before the Commission. It involves a group of gas distributors known as the Transco customer group, which consists of eleven major private distributor companies (among the largest are Brooklyn Union Gas Co., Consolidated Edison, Long Island Lighting, Public Service Electric and Gas, Washington Gas Light, and Atlantic Gas Light). The distributor companies propose to form a new corporation—Beneficial Exploration and Development Corporation (BEDCO)—to explore and develop onshore gas supplies. Transcontinental Gas Pipe Line Company will impose a $.03 surcharge on all firm sales and will act as a conduit and return these funds to BEDCO for the domestic exploration and development program. It is estimated that the surcharge on consumers will provide approximately $27 million annually.

It is interesting to note that major opposition to the use of the surcharge arrangement was filed by Mobil, Phillips Petroleum, and Exxon Corporation. The producers contended, among other things, that the proposal is discriminatory and anticompetitive because it provided risk-free capital to a nonprofit corporation (BEDCO) which would outbid its competitors for attractive leases as well as realize other special advantages.

While one of the producers, Inexco Oil Co., did not object to the surcharge concept, it did oppose the BEDCO plan. Inexco suggested that instead of the distribution companies obtaining surcharge funds, such an arrangement should be implemented for the independent producers. Subsequently, Inexco petitioned the FPC for a rulemaking (RP74-79), proposing a $.03 exploration surcharge on all gas transported in interstate commerce with the proceeds going directly to producers. The additional cost to consumers of this proposal, if implemented, would approach $400 million annually.

In another proceeding, Pacific Gas Transmission (PGT) (RP73-111) proposes to amend its gas purchase contract with its Canadian supplier, Alberta and Southern Gas Company Ltd., to increase the price paid at the Canadian border by $.01 per Mcf in order to establish a fund for exploration and development of gas supplies in Canada. The resultant new supplies, of course, are to be committed to Alberta and Southern.

One interesting aspect of this proposal is the affiliate relationship that exists between Pacific Gas Transmission and Alberta and Southern Gas Company and the parent, Pacific Gas and Electric Company (PG&E). Alberta and Southern Gas Company is wholly owned by PG&E, and in addition the latter owns a 52.7 percent interest in Pacific Gas Transmission. The funds collected by the surcharge proposed by Pacific Gas Transmission would provide interest-free capital to an affiliate and obviously benefit the parent, PG&E.

The staff opposed the Pacific Gas Transmission surcharge plan, but did not take any position on the former BEDCO proposal. They objected to the PGT proposal because there was no assurance of the availability of these Canadian supplies within a reasonable period of time. In addition, the staff contended that PGT failed to justify the surcharge as a "cost" normally associated with a utility's cost of service, and objected to the duration of the surcharge to 1986.

The fundamental question that arises regarding all these arrangements to shift the risk from private business to consumers through the use of a surcharge concerns a number of probing equity questions. If consumers are to provide the risk capital, should not the benefits also be shared by them? An additional related problem concerns the effect of backward integration by distributors on arm's-length bargaining and the general question of viable competitive market structure in the natural gas industry.

Backward Integration of Private Distribution Companies

While the surcharge may be the financial vehicle in which private distribution company systems seek to enter the production stage, the broader market structure implications are far more significant. In the past, gas distribution companies whose primary pursuit was the sale of gas in the end market would further their own self-interests by vigorously opposing unjustifiable price requests by producers in area rate and other proceedings before the Commission. With the current gas shortage, the sole concern of gas distributors is to attach new supplies, and their opposition to producer price demands has evaporated. Obviously, the capitulation to producers' demands will be more complete in those instances where the distributor is also a producer and where the prospects for profit maximization exist at both levels.

In addition to the BEDCO group discussed previously, the formation of seven utilities, the New York Gas Group (NYGAS)[b] will also utilize a surcharge to raise funds for exploration and development. This proposal to facilitate backward integration was approved by the New York Public Service Commission in August 1973. In this instance, the NYGAS group will participate in a joint venture with Tenneco Oil Company for the acquisition of offshore leases.

The FPC response to this recent major backward integration by distributors is reflected in a case involving a wholly owned subsidiary of Consumers Power Co., Northern Michigan Exploration Company (NOMECO).[16] The Commission concluded that the arrangements proposed were not objectionable as a matter of law or policy and that the benefits of the project were fully supported. They said, "Consumers [Power Co.] needs gas for its customers; NOMECO, in concert with

[b]Members of the Group are Brooklyn Union Gas Co., Central Hudson Gas & Electric Corp., Consolidated Edison Co. of New York, Iroquois Gas Corp., Long Island Lighting Co., New York State Electric & Gas Corp., and Orange & Rockland Utilities, Inc.

others, and with the financing from its parent, has found it. No argument presented to us persuades us that Consumers should be foreclosed from enjoying the fruits of NOMECO's success."

At the same time that the Commission affirmed the NOMECO proposal, it approved the arrangement of Elizabethtown Gas Company's application.[17] In this instance, Elizabethtown, through its wholly owned subsidiary, National Exploration, had arranged for the transportation by Transcontinental of supplies from its affiliate for its own use.

There are a number of very basic factors underlying the distributor backward integration to the production function. First, because of the lack of geological and geophysical expertise, the gas distributor companies find it advantageous to participate with existing producers in the acquisition of leases and in the exploration and development of new supplies. Second, these supplies are always tied to the distribution company's own system and by-pass the general commitment to the pipeline system in which the needs of all customers are considered.

In fact, this was the basis for the opposition to the Elizabethtown and NOMECO proposals by Central Illinois Light Company. The FPC staff and Central Illinois objected to the Elizabethtown proposal because the distributor, by "tying in" the new gas supply to its own system, would provide the means for discrimination against the smaller distribution systems which do not have the financial ability to become producers. In addition, one of the most serious aspects of any extensive backward integration by distributors is the potential undermining of the arm's-length bargaining that existed in the past, and the related threat to buyer-seller independence which is so important in seeking a more viable and competitive market structure.

Related Developments

There are additional proposals currently before the Federal Power Commission which reflect the desire to shift the operational and financial risks to the consumers. One of the issues reserved in a Natural Gas Pipeline Co. of America rate settlement (Docket No. RP73-110) is the propriety of including coal lease payments in the company's cost of service. In connection with the planned construction of a coal gasification plant in North Dakota, Natural Gas Pipeline obtained the rights to certain coal reserves. The company proposes to include $500,000 per year of coal option payments in its rate base. They contend that the payments are directly related to its existing and future business of providing reliable gas service.

The FPC staff opposes the inclusion of option payments in the rate base because the coal feedstock is to be used in a nonjurisdictional facility, and assuming that the payments are jurisdictional expenditures that any benefit to consumers have not been demonstrated. In addition, the staff contends that there is no assurance that the plant will ever be constructed, and if built, it will not be operational before 1982. Last, the staff pointed out that there is no guarantee that the coal involved in this instance will ever be mined.

It is ironic that in this same case the staff opposed the inclusion of $157 million of a lump-sum advance payment in the settlement proposal. They contend that the advances would not be fully utilized by the producers until 1 or 2 years after they are made, at a minimum. The staff concluded that the ratepayers should not be burdened with the cost of these advance payments which are not currently needed by producers and which may never be required if initial exploration proves further development unwarranted.

In a related development, Southern Natural Gas Co. petitioned the Commission (Docket No. RP74-93, filed May 15, 1974) to issue a declaratory order which provided that the cost of acquiring certain coal reserves be dedicated to a coal gasification plant appropriate for inclusion in rate base (Account 105, Gas Plant Held for Future Use). In the petition, Southern Natural explained that they had entered an agreement with Consolidation Coal Co. for a 2-year exclusive option to purchase about half of the "Hillsboro" coal reserves in the Illinois basin, covering approximately 273 million tons of recoverable coal. Southern Natural said that the 2-year option period is specifically designed to allow FPC authorization to include coal payments in the rate base. They insist that assurance is necessary prior to the purchase and that the investment in coal reserves is a proper rate base item. The company contends that the Commission's disclaimer of jurisdiction over coal gasification facilities is no bar to rate base treatment of its investment in coal reserves. Last, Southern Natural insists that financing the coal gasification facilities is infeasible unless they are granted this assurance prior to any Section 4 (under the Natural Gas Act) justification of the rates.

One facet of the Commission's position on these issues is reflected in the modification of a settlement offer made by Michigan Wisconsin Pipe Line Co. (Docket No. RP73-102). In an order dated June 26, 1974, the Commission rejected the inclusion in the cost of service of approximately $1.1 million in delayed rental payments for coal leases associated with a proposed coal gasification program. They agreed with the staff that there is no assurance that the coal will be mined or gasified. Therefore, "the possible benefit is too far removed from the costs proposed to be borne by the natural gas consumer."

In another distinct but related problem area mentioned previously, El Paso Natural Gas Co. (Docket No. RP69-6) proposed to use the $31.5 million of excess revenues collected above the "just and reasonable" rates for an exploration and development fund.[c] The only pipeline customer objecting to the retention of these excess rates and charges is Nevada Power Co. Since the distributors would have to flow the refunds through to ultimate consumers, the potential benefits to these distributors of additional supplies appear to outweigh the conventional claim by consumers to funds they have paid in excess of reasonable rates.

The danger of such a precedent is that it will prompt every pipeline company with a producing affiliate (and this includes all the major interstate pipeline companies) to make a claim for refunds which legitimately should be returned to consumers. In addition, it provides the incipient danger that future pipeline rate increase filings will be inflated in hopes that the excess revenues collected can be retained as interest-free funds for exploration and development.

Conclusion

The foregoing analysis illustrates a great variety of significant changes in the formulation of and the ultimate decisions concerning public policy. While a clear-cut separation cannot be drawn between business risk and financial risk, it is apparent that such proposals as the volume variation adjustment clause (VVAC), the use of the purchase gas adjustment procedure, the inclusion of option payments and delay rentals on coal reserves, the assured return of investment in coal gasification facilities, and retention of pipelines of revenues above just and reasonable rates for exploration and development primarily reflect a transference of operational risk from the enterprise to the consumer. The use of advance payments and the surcharge on consumer rates reflect, in large measure, a shift of financial risk from the firm to the ratepayer.

Despite the transfer in many instances of operational and financial risk of the enterprise to the ratepayer, there has been no recognition of this fact in the determination of a rate of return for the firm. In addition, it must be recognized that the extent to which automatic adjustments to the cost of service are permitted reflects a relaxation of regulatory review and control that may not serve the public interest.

Another facet of the current developments associated with the unavailability of natural gas supplies from conventional sources is the resultant problems associated with curtailments and the development of high-cost supplemental supplies. The Commission's determination to use incremental pricing for these higher-cost sources has been opposed by the pipeline companies and distributors. In contrast to the major communications car-

---

[c]This proposal was approved by the Commission (see Order on Rehearing issued August 26, 1974).

rier, the pipeline industry opposes incremental cost pricing for business reasons. The lesson that can be drawn from this parallel is that the firm does not support or oppose incremental pricing because of allocative efficiency or equity but because of the advantages of market strategy.

Finally, the backward integration of gas distributors has many serious market structure implications which vitiate the countervailing power that has been a strong ally for consumer protection in the past.

Producer Regulation

Introduction

The alternatives concerning producer regulation reflect the polar extremes of public policy. Currently, there is a bill (S. 371) before the Senate Commerce Committee which would exempt all producer sales from well-head regulation. In contrast, the administration's bill (S. 2048) proposes to deregulate "new" gas sales. The definition of "new" sales under this bill is gas dedicated for the first time or rededicated upon the expiration of an existing contract after April 15, 1973, or produced from wells commenced after this date. Last, the bills sponsored by Senators Magnuson and Stevenson would extend FPC jurisdiction to wellhead regulation of intra-state sales and would strengthen and expand FPC authority. An additional provision of this bill (S. 2506) recognizes the need to inject more competition in the petroleum industry. It proposes to establish a federal oil and gas corporation to engage in exploration, development, and production of oil and gas on federal lands.

The divergence of the objectives of the various bills reflects the wide variety of views held with regard to the market structure of the natural gas-producing industry. It is this fundamental determination which provides the rationale for deregulation or continued and expanded regulation in any objective assessment of public policy alternatives.

Producer Prices

On April 11, 1973, the Commission initiated a nationwide rulemaking (R-389-B) to establish nationwide rates for all jurisdictional sales from wells commenced after January 1, 1973. Opinion No. 699 (issued June 21, 1974) established a single uniform nationwide base rate of $.42 per Mcf (exclusive of state production taxes) for contracts executed and sales commenced after January 1, 1973. In addition, the new gas price will apply to gas formerly certificated (permanently) under contracts which had expired by their own terms on or after January 1, 1973.

The $.42 national base rate is applicable to both casinghead gas and dry gas. In addition, Opinion 699 provided for a fixed-price annual escalation of $.01 per Mcf, beginning on January 1, 1974, a Btu upward and downward price adjustment based on 1,000 Btu, an allowance for production taxes (plus any increase), and a gathering allowance dependent upon the producing area.

The rate is to remain in effect until June 30, 1976 (or earlier, as may be modified by the Commission). In addition, the Commission provided for a biennial review of the national rate with the initial review commencing on or after January 1, 1975.

The Commission simultaneously rescinded a number of short-term pricing procedures when it prescribed the new nationwide rate, including the termination of limited-term and 60-day emergency sales. The opinion noted that these procedures accounted for nearly 48 percent of the new deliveries in the interstate market during 1971-1973. The Commission concluded that this proportion was inordinately high and should be reduced in order to encourage long-term dedications.

In addition to the cost-based area rate procedures for wellhead prices, the Commission has utilized a number of pricing procedures in which market factors are also price determinants. One of the earliest procedures was the emergency sales for periods up to 60 days without any formal certificate authorization or rate review requirements.[18] Another pricing alternative available to producers was the limited-term certificate procedure in which the Commission has approved contract prices above area ceilings, usually for a 1-year period, with pregranted abandonment. Producers have filed for limited-term certificate sales predominantly in the range of $.60 to $.65 per Mcf with a top price of $.70. The maximum price permitted by the Commission for a limited-term sale was $.50 per Mcf.

In late 1973, the Commission modified its earlier emergency order and extended the 60-day emergency sale procedures to permit for emergency sales of up to 180 days.[19] Sales reported under this latter emergency procedure reflect a weighted average price of $.5999 per Mcf as of May 13, 1974. The highest price sale was $.75 per Mcf paid by Panhandle Eastern Pipe Line Company. Order No. 491 has been challenged by a number of consumer groups and members of Congress on the contention that it is administrative deregulaton. Recently, the Commission discontinued the 180-day emergency sales beyond March 15, 1974, pending a review for the need to reinstitute these sales in the future.

In another precedent-making decision, the Commission has exempted small producer rates from direct regulation.[20] In this instance, the Commission determined that producers selling less than 10 million Mcf annually in interstate commerce did not have to file their rates with the Commission for approval. The Commission provided for a review of the rates paid by pipeline purchasers to the small producers in the pipelines' cost of service and for disallowance if determined unreasonable.

As a basis for guidance to the interstate pipeline companies, the Commission indicated it would look at the prices being paid in the intrastate market and the highest prices paid by other interstate pipeline companies at that time. The U.S. Supreme Court on June 10, 1974, partially reversed the Washington D.C. Circuit decision and affirmed the FPC's determination to regulate small producers indirectly. The Court remanded the case to the Commission because of the failure to provide a mechanism for ensuring that small-producer rates would be just and reasonable. The Court explicitly rejected the exclusive reliance on market prices as a final basis for the determination of appropriate rates.

Finally, the Commission provided another pricing avenue, in this instance for commitments of long-term contract supplies, when it established the optional pricing procedure.[21] This optional procedure for permanent certification of new gas sales provides for rates in excess of area ceilings, among other considerations, when "special circumstances" are shown to permit the Commission to judge whether the contract rate is just and reasonable. One of the factors considered by the Commission is the following:

The seller-applicant for an optional procedure certificate must state the ground for claiming that issuance of such certificate is in the public convenience and necessity, and must provide "factual support" for such claim. Further, the purchaser involved must also certify that the certificate is required by the present or future public convenience and necessity and, in addition, provide information (by incorporation from information already in the FPC files, where possible) respecting systemwide supply, present and estimated three-year daily and annual requirements, deliverability life, implementation of any curtailment plans, emergency purchases of gas, and purchases of LNG or attachment of other supplemental supplies.

A number of parties have challenged the optional pricing procedure in the court. Among them are the Consumer Federation of America, 21 Concerned Congressmen, the American Public Gas Association, and the New York Commission, contending that the procedure amounts to deregulation. The highest price permitted by the Commission under the optional pricing procedure is $.55 per Mcf.[22]

The Washington D.C. Circuit Court of Appeals affirmed the Commission's use of optional pricing in a recent decision.[23] Pointing to the shortage of available gas supply and the curtailments of firm customers, the Court agreed to the pricing procedures as a premise for new supply elicitation. In addition, the Court rejected the petitioners' contention that the

Commission was using contract prices arrived at between producers and pipeline companies for establishing just and reasonable rates. They pointed out that the Commission provided for individual hearings in which "just and reasonable" rate standards are applied to each certificate case. In addition, the Court said:

> . . . the Commission's review will include consideration of costs; and since all applications are subject to notice, intervention and hearings, all parties are free, upon a "showing of special circumstances" to challenge the cost findings embodied in area rate decisions.

In testimony[24] before the Senate Committee on Commerce, Chairperson John N. Nassikas indicated the 1973 range of volumes and prices of all new natural gas sales committed to the interstate market under the various pricing procedures (see Table 3-1).

An assessment of the commitments in 1973 under the various pricing procedures reflected in this table, if the small-producer sales are omitted, indicates that there has been a marked shift to short-term sales. Approximately 65 percent of the deliveries were of a short-term nature.

Another important consideration relates to the commitments under long-term area rate contracts in 1972 of approximately 527 Bcf (billion cubic feet) in contrast to deliveries in 1973 of 265 Bcf (as shown in the table). For southern Louisiana, in the post-Second Round Opinion 598, the drop was from 309.6 Bcf in 1972 to 146.6 Bcf in 1973. The evidence indicates a drastic shift to short-term, higher-priced commitments to the interstate market under these various pricing procedures, and away from longer-term, lower-priced sales under area rates.

I have indicated in earlier congressional testimony the anomalous relationship (negative elasticity) between price and new supplies.[25] A comparison of new reserve additions in the 5-year period from 1963 to 1967 indicates average annual additions of 20.3 Tcf (trillion cubic feet), in contrast to 10.5 Tcf in the latter 5-year period from 1968 to 1972. Over this same time frame, the weighted initial contract price increased by approximately one-third, but new supply additions were 50 percent *lower* in the latter period. The weighted average new area ceiling price increased by one-third from 1968 to 1972, but new supply additions *fell* about 30 percent.

An examination of recent price increases and reserve additions indicates that this inverse relationship has continued. In July 1971, the Commission established an area rate ceiling for new gas in southern Louisiana of $.26 per Mcf and in May 1973 approved a price of $.45 per Mcf in the Belco proceeding. This reflects a price increase of over 73 percent in less than 2 years. In addition, in February 1974 (less than 1 year after the Belco case), the Commission approved a price of $.55 per Mcf (an increase of over 22 percent above the Belco price) in the sale by Mallard Exploration, Inc., to

Table 3-1
Volume and Price Range for New Interstate Natural Gas Sales Under Various Pricing Procedures During 1973

Pricing Procedure	Deliveries (Mcf)	Average Price (Mcf)
Area rate ceilings	265,000,000	24.63
Optional procedure	87,000,000	39.93
Limited-term sales	340,000,000	40.85
Small-producer sales	107,000,000	42.43
60-day emergency sales	116,000,000	46.11
180-day emergency sales	201,000,000	50.41
Total	1,116,000,000	Avg. 39.35

Southern Natural Gas Company (Docket No. 73-154). In response to these significant price increases, the reserves added *dropped* about 30 percent from approximately 9.4 Tcf in 1972 to 6.5 Tcf in 1973.

What appears to be a basic contradiction can be explained very simply: this is a market where the major producers can seriously constrain development and commitments of new supplies. It is apparent that gas producers would prefer to speculate that deregulation or price increases in the future will result in higher returns (at the discounted present value) than the current rate of return.

The Natural Gas-Producer Market

The advocates of price deregulation of wellhead gas contend that the gas-producing industry is workably competitive because of the following factors:

1. The large numbers of producers
2. The alleged existence of arm's-length bargaining
3. The bargaining power of pipeline companies
4. The low measure of concentration in contrast to other industry sectors
5. The alleged low entry barriers

In the initial area rate proceedings, the Commission examined the evidence provided by the gas-producing industry to support their contention that competition was adequate to permit the use of contract prices as a regulatory guide for area rates. The earlier Commission determination was to rely upon cost-based rates, and they rejected the industry's claim that the market structure was workably competitive.

In contrast, in Opinion No. 659 (Belco Petroleum Corporation), issued

May 30, 1973, the Commission concluded that "There is no evidence that intra- or interstate gas contract prices are tainted with anticompetitive conduct by gas producers."

In the Belco proceeding, the staff presented evidence that the producer market structure was not effectively competitive and that market criteria were inappropriate as a regulatory standard. They argued for the use of cost-based rates as a means of overcoming the affiliate relationship between Tenneco Oil and Tennessee Gas Pipeline, and stressed the use of costs as an essential ingredient in continued producer regulation. The empirical evidence introduced by the staff indicated conclusively the oligopolistic market structure of the natural gas-producer industry and addressed the following factors:

1. Concentration over "new" gas supplies
2. Interlocking relationships among major producers and between major producers and smaller independent companies
3. Interlocking relationships between producers and purchasing pipeline companies
4. The existence of major bidding combinations in offshore lease sales
5. Individual and bank director interlocks between major petroleum companies
6. The dual role of the major producers as intrastate purchasers of gas for their own pipeline systems and sellers of gas in the interstate market.

Concentration over Supply

An examination of information concerning natural gas production indicates that 22 domestic producers supplied the interstate pipelines with 71 percent of the gas in 1971. This would appear to be a relatively low measure of concentration, *assuming* that it is an appropriate guide to control over supply. The truth is that the bulk of the gas produced in any one year has been committed to contract many years in the past, and only a small fraction could be considered "new" supply. Therefore, unlike other industry sectors, the production in any one year is not indicative of new supplies, and the concentration measure cannot relate to this year's output.

Studies by the Office of Economics (FPC) indicate that the eight-firm concentration over supply measured on the basis of new gas contracts for the period 1965-1970 in fact indicated significant concentration. For southern Louisiana, the eight-firm concentration ranged between 61 percent and 86 percent in this period, in the Permian Basin between 76 percent and 94 percent, and between 72 percent and 99 percent in the Texas Gulf Coast in any one year.

Table 3-2
Four and Eight Firm Concentration Ratios for Major Offshore Lease Sales of Natural Gas, 1970-1974

	Four-firm Concentration[a]	Eight-firm Concentration[a]
December 15, 1970	50.6%	71.8%
September 12, 1972	76.7	96.5
December 19, 1972	48.7	75.1
June 19, 1973	74.6	87.0
December 20, 1973	80.4	93.3
March 28, 1974	49.0	71.7

[a]Bid Recap Sheets, Bureau of Land Management, Department of the Interior, Oil and Gas Lease Sale for date indicated.

In terms of anticipatory supplies, the concentration ratios on the basis of bonuses paid for offshore leases also indicate significant concentration. The four- and eight-firm concentration for the major offshore lease sales are as shown in Table 3-2. An examination of the evidence presented, using any meaningful measure of concentration over "new" gas supplies, indicates significant control by the major producers.

Interlocking Relationships among Major Producers and between Major Producers and Smaller Independent Companies

An examination of the evidence filed in formal proceedings by the Office of Economics indicates that only four of sixteen major producers with an interest in the federal offshore domain own 50 percent or more of their producing leases independently. In contrast, ten of the sixteen own 80 percent or more of the offshore properties jointly with one another. In addition, it is significant to note that very few companies outside of the top sixteen have any independent holdings at all.

An examination of the ownership of onshore producing leases in the state of Louisiana is a further indication of highly interconnected arrangements. Of the eighteen largest major producers, fourteen have five or more direct interlocks with the other seventeen. For example, Continental Oil has 28 joint ventures with Arco, 27 with Cities Service, 27 with Getty, 16 with Mobil, 13 with Exxon, and 11 each with Amoco and Sun. In addition, the 38 other medium-sized and large-sized producers holding Louisiana leases showed substantial interlocking ownership arrangements with the majors. Another force prompting interlocking interdependence is the state conservation measures requiring unitization of gas fields.

Interlocking Relationships between Producers and Purchasing Pipelines

An examination of the buying side illustrates another blockage to workable competition because all major pipeline purchasers have producing affiliates. This all-pervasive backward integration by pipelines is one of the most cogent factors blocking meaningful bargaining between producers and pipeline companies. The fact that pipelines can automatically pass on the cost of purchased gas provides little incentive for vigorous bargaining to obtain the lowest possible price. Obviously, any increase in the price of gas which is paid by pipeline companies to producers can be used as a justification for higher price requests for gas from their own producing affiliates. In this way, profit margins for the parent firm can be enhanced both at the production level and at the transmission phase of the business.

Another indication of the blockage to meaningful competition between pipeline companies and producers is the participation by interstate pipeline company affiliates in offshore lease acquisitions with major producers. For example, in the March 28, 1974, offshore Louisiana lease sale, pipeline-producing affiliates were successful bidders on approximately one-half the leases in this sale. In every instance, the pipeline affiliate participated with the majors and other producers in the acquisition of these leases. It is obvious that the joint ownership and subsequent production from jointly held acreage undermines the assumed independence in buyer-seller transactions that are essential for a competitive market. This "community of interests" between the pipeline companies and their producing partners is irrefutable evidence of an unworkably competitive market in the gas producer sector.

The Existence of Major Bidding Combinations in Offshore Lease Sales

Further evidence of interdependence concerns the major bidding combinations reflected in offshore lease sales. Because the majors belong to two or more of these combines, the web of interdependence is far more extensive than would be indicated by the membership in any single combination. Here again, the extensive participation by affiliates of major interstate gas pipeline companies with producers in these bidding combines for offshore federal leases provides cogent evidence of their mutual interest.

Individual and Bank Director Interlocks among Major Petroleum Companies

A recent article in *The New York Times* (March 12, 1974) indicated that the

Justice Department and the Federal Trade Commission are investigating a number of individuals who serve on the board of directors of two or more petroleum companies. There is also evidence of individuals serving as directors on the boards of pipeline companies as well as on those of petroleum companies.

In addition, there is substantial evidence that representatives from various financial institutions serve as directors on boards of two or more petroleum companies. For example, the First National City Bank has representatives serving as directors on the boards of Exxon, Mobil Oil, Sinclair Oil, Allied Chemical, Monsanto Co., and W.R. Grace Co. Obviously, when representatives from various banking institutions serve on two or more boards, we cannot expect vigorous rivalry among petroleum companies which have this type of interlock.

In addition, there may be some question as to whether a financial institution with a vested interest in one or more petroleum companies would freely provide capital to an existing or potential competitor since this action could adversely affect the firm or firms in which the bank has an interest. This problem has dual implications: first, with regard to barriers for competition and new entry, and, second, as to the availability of capital to expand exploration, development, and production to meet our energy requirements.

The Dual Role of the Major Producers as Intrastate Purchasers of Gas for Their Pipeline Systems and Sellers of Gas in the Interstate Market

Another anticompetitive characteristic concerns the fact that major producers purchase gas for their intrastate pipeline systems and sell gas to interstate pipeline companies. Such majors as Exxon (Monterey Pipeline), Texaco, Continental Oil, and Phillips Petroleum have extensive intrastate pipeline networks. By paying higher prices for their own gas, or taking gas from wells in which they have a working interest, or by using gas purchased in the intrastate market the major producers use these prices for their demands for higher prices for their sales in the interstate market. This dual role of buyer-seller by the major petroleum companies undermines the essential independence required for intercorporate rivalry and fundamental to the assumption of a workably competitive market.

Recent FPC Proceedings

In hearings before the Commission, new evidence demonstrates the lack of arm's-length bargaining as well as the ability of the producer to administer prices. In the Louisiana Land and Exploration Company proceeding (Docket No. CI73-501), evidence was introduced which showed that the management of the pipeline purchaser, Texas Eastern, and the selling producer, Louisiana Land, were interlocked. It is noteworthy that Texas Eastern Exploration Company, a wholly owned subsidiary of Texas Eastern Transmission Corp., is a partner with Louisiana Land and other producers in the ownership of federal offshore leases.

The lack of arm's-length bargaining and the problems of relying upon contract prices in the sale by a producing affiliate to a pipeline affiliate were clearly demonstrated in the Pennzoil Producing Company proceeding (Docket No. CI72-321). In the course of cross-examination, the pipeline company witness admitted that in the initial contract, the producing affiliate agreed to sell gas to United Gas Pipe Line Company at $.30 per Mcf in 1971. This contract was subsequently abrogated, and a new contract was signed in 1972 for $.35 per Mcf. The justification provided by the witness was that an unwritten agreement provided that if the "independent" producers who were part of the joint venture could obtain a higher price, then the pipeline company would pay the same price and would extend the same terms and conditions to its own affiliate. It is obvious that the lack of arm's-length bargaining, and in this instance the restraint of trade implications in unwritten agreements of this nature, taints the negotiations whenever a pipeline producer affiliate is involved.

Another example of market constraint was apparent in a recent application by Atlantic Richfield Company (Docket No. CI73-691) for a limited-term certificate. The ability of the company to administer the price of gas is readily apparent. In his initial decision, the administrative law judge stated that:

Arco's witness testified that Texas Eastern Transmission Company bid 55¢ per Mcf for this gas. When asked why that bid was not preferred to the one that was accepted, he answered that Arco believed that the Commission would approve a 50¢ price without a hearing.

He further commented that:

The above passage exemplifies some, but not all, of Arco's desire to avoid regulation that this record shows. It shows that United Gas Pipe Line, which was in a far more severe curtailment situation than Trunkline, made a bid identical to Trunkline's. The bid was refused because Arco learned that United expected its customers to intervene before the Commission in opposition to such a sale. Trunkline indicated that there would be no opposition and in fact there was none.

Last, in another proceeding before the Commission involving Okmar Oil Company (Docket No. CI73-707), the witness for the company was asked what he would do if his application to sell gas to Northern Natural

Gas Company at $.61 per Mcf were denied. The witness responded that he could commit the gas to intrastate commerce or, he said, "The second alternative would be to not to market the gas at all." He concluded:

And then we have a third alternative which is a matter of some discussion. Uncommitted gas reserves now are apparently among the finest assets that a company can have—an independent gas producing company—and we are constantly, repeatedly, not only with respect to this property but with respect to any reserves we have—we are being contacted by other gas producing companies, independent(s), and majors, who are interested in buying the reserves in situ. They have expressed their willingness to bid on the come, so to speak, to take the gamble that the reserves would appreciate in the ground.

In denying the certificate application, the administrative law judge, in his findings and conclusions given from the bench (August 2, 1973), said, "Furthermore, Northern has a measurable interest in gas reserves, and would indirectly benefit from price increases."

The facts in this case indicate that Northern has acreage surrounding the Okmar properties, and it would be naïve to expect that they would bargain vigorously in purchasing Okmar supplies (perhaps this is indicated by the price level offered). Obviously, as producer-sellers, they benefit from high prices, and as pipeline purchasers, there is very little disadvantage because of the ability to collect the higher prices paid with minimal lag.

Conclusion: Evidence on Market Structure

The evidence presented on both the buying side and the selling side of the natural gas-producer market leads to the inescapable conclusion that the market imperfections are so all-pervasive that they render competition unworkable. It is apparent from the institutional arrangements depicted in this analysis that the assertion of the natural gas producers that large numbers of firms and low entry barriers assure a competitive market structure is not supported by the empirical evidence. These assertions fail to recognize that the small independent sellers are unable to enter the prolific offshore areas independently, or at all, because of substantial investment requirements. The entry of small producers cannot be characterized as inducing competitive interplay when they depend on farm-outs by the major producers (who retain a working interest or buy out the independent who is successful in the discovery of gas or other hydrocarbons). In addition, the smaller independent producers will enter into joint ventures with the larger producers, which results in a coalescence of their interests. Last, new entrants have inadequate market power to offset the dominance of the majors and rarely influence supply or price in an independent manner.

The extensive areas of interdependence and commonality of interests among producers preclude rivalry and competitive interplay. The implications for competition and new entry as well as reasonable prices are clear, in that the public interest would not be served by deregulation in a market manifesting these characteristics.

Notes

1. Order No. 452 (R-406), issued April 14, 1972.

2. Opinion No. 699, issued June 21, 1974.

3. Opinion 622, 47 FPC 1624 and Opinion No. 622-A, 48 FPC 723.

4. Opinion No. 671, issued October 31, 1973.

5. Opinion No. 600 issued August 23, 1971, and Opinion No. 600-A issued May 8, 1972.

6. Testimony of Dr. Rodney E. Stevenson, United Gas Pipe Line Company, Docket No. RP74-21, March 14, 1974.

7. Orders No. 467 and 467-B issued March 2, 1973, and Order No. 467-C issued April 4, 1974.

8. *Texas Gulf, Inc. v. F.P.C.,* Petition No. 72-3597, May 31, 1974.

9. Requirements and Curtailments of Major Interstate Pipeline Companies Based on Form 16 Reports, June 1974.

10. Opinion No. 622, issued June 28, 1972.

11. Opinion No. 637, issued December 7, 1972.

12. Opinion No. 663, issued September 24, 1973.

13. Testimony of FPC staff witness Dr. Rodney E. Stevenson, January 25, 1974, Docket No. CP73-131.

14. Order No. 499 (Docket No. RM74-4), issued December 28, 1973.

15. Opinion No. 684, issued January 31, 1974.

16. Opinion No. 668-A, issued December 7, 1973.

17. Opinion No. 678, issued December 7, 1973.

18. Order No. 418, issued December 10, 1970.

19. Order No. 491, issued September 14, 1973.

20. Order No. 428-C, issued April 10, 1972.

21. Order No. 455, issued August 3, 1972.

22. Opinion No. 686, issued February 1, 1974.

23. John E. Moss, et al., *Petitioners v. Federal Power Commission,* Respondent, No. 72-1837; American Public Gas Association, American Public Power Association, Consumer Federation of America' *Petitioners v. Federal Power Commission,* Respondent, No. 72-1846, decided August 15, 1974.

24. Summary Statement of John N. Nassikas, Chairman, FPC, U.S. Senate Committee on Commerce, February 19, 1974.

25. Hearings before the Special Subcommittee on Integrated Oil Operations of the Committee on Interior and Insular Affairs, United States Senate, *Market Performance and Competition in the Petroleum Industry,* Part 3, December 12 and 13, 1973. Hearing before the Subcommittee on Antitrust and Monopoly of the Committee on the Judiciary, United States Senate, *The Natural Gas Industry,* Part I, June 26, 27, and 28, 1973.

4

The Structure of Utility Rates

John Monsees

My responsibility in the rate area is parceling out the total costs to the different customers. That is, I design the rate structure. It's the job of deciding how the revenue needs of the company will be divided among the service classifications, and more important for the subject today, how it will be divided among small-, medium-, and large-size customers. So it's a little bit different from what we talked about before, that is, keeping the whole utility solvent.

Nobody likes higher rates any more than the next fellow, and low promotional rates were especially popular several years ago. Even as late as 1970, a marketing executive was saying, "Remember, marketing is the surest answer to the increased revenue needs of your companies to face the ever-increasing demands for capacity and environmental protection."[1] And the Federal Power Commission has issued a report which listed some nine different types of promotional devices. Promotional rates were among them and also installation allowances, conversion allowances, service allowances, merchandising allowances, advertising allowances, financing assistance, cash payments, and even something called "other" allowances. The executive I mentioned referred to these nine different allowances and devices and added that "all of them . . . seem to be coming under closer scrutiny both within and without your companies."[2] Well, that's been more and more true since that statement was made. Many, if not most, programs have been curtailed or discontinued either on the utility's own initiative or at the direction of a regulatory commission. Even while this marketing executive was talking about ever-increasing demands for capacity, an FPC official was saying that with energy supply and distribution in conflict with environmental values, we are increasingly offered the solution that "society should forego that particular increment of power supply . . . that continued growth is not necessarily in man's long-run best interest."[3]

What's happened since that time? A North Carolina company has been engaged in promotional advertising. In mid-1971 the North Carolina Commission advised the utility that future promotional advertising expenses should be kept at an absolute minimum. Also in mid-1971, seasonal rate differentials were being introduced around the country, providing for higher rates during the summer and lower rates during the winter for those companies which had a summer peaking load. The Pennsylvania Commission commented that rates should be based on "the hard economic facts of life."[4] At about that time another commission held that residential customers should have the privilege of making their own selection of the type of energy to be used on the basis of cost, and not to be overly influenced by promotional rates. Now what did they mean by "cost"? The article reviewing this decision goes on to say that, "Thus an electric company was directed to adjust its proposed schedules so that all residential electric customers would pay the same rate for like quantities of energy used, regardless of how the energy is consumed."[5] In this instance, cost is being equated to charging the same amount for the same quantity used regardless of load characteristics which determine time and manner of use.

What are some of the other things that have happened since then? Time-of-day metering is being proposed in order to give a different price for off-peak and on-peak electricity, that is, for electricity generated from base load versus peak load units. Another is conservation. Conservation took hold. Our customers decreased their use of service. Our fixed costs stayed the same while use decreased, and the result is higher rates, to cover the fixed costs. Not a very popular happening, but a cost-related one nevertheless.

Now back to the theme. I'm not going to try to tell you whether promotional rates should continue to exist, or whether they are justified. But I'd just like to give you my candid view of where I think the electric industry is going to be heading in terms of its rate design, as it spreads its revenue needs among the different customers. It seems to me the industry is heading in the direction of cost-based rates. Now that may not seem startling, but the fact is that many of today's rates and many in the past have not been entirely cost-based. But I believe that we're heading toward a time when, spread across the spectrum of classifications and the different sizes of customers, rates will be made more cost-based. Summer-winter rate differentials, time-of-day rates, and the revenue effects of conservation are examples of the trend.

If the utility industry follows the direction I have assumed what will the structure of the rates look like? Will they still look promotional, or will they not look promotional? Will they be virtually flat? Will they be inverted? Or will there be decreasing unit charges for larger customers? Graduated rates having decreasing unit charges for increasing consumption have been the norm of the electric utility industry. They have come under severe attack. Graduated rates have been equated in the minds of many people with promotional rates. "They're inherently promotional, not cost-related" is the cry. When this subject is broached, I've found that I have to leave behind all my preconceptions because the answers don't always come out the way I think they will.

Let's look for a minute at the elements of cost. I want to look at four different types or classes of customers. Let's look at residential customers, small commercial customers, large commercial customers, and residential apartment buildings. The cost of service to these customers is divided into customer cost, demand cost, and energy cost. The *customer costs* are the costs associated with metering and billing the customer, the cost of the service line into the building, and a portion of the distribution system cost. These are the costs which are incurred whether any use is actually made of the service. They are incurred because the customer exists at a specific location and must be connected into the central station system. The *demand costs* are the costs generally associated with plant. They are the fixed costs of ownership of the production, transmission, and distribution plant. They exclude those plant costs associated with the customer component. The demand costs include a portion of the production costs where these costs are fixed in nature and do not vary with the volume of kilowatthours produced. These would be such items as the fuel necessary to keep a generator spinning on the line and certain lubricating costs. The *energy costs* are the truly variable costs of producing power. These consist mainly of the cost of fuel used in producing power.

Now if we divide our cost on that basis, what do we come up with? Let's look at the electric business as a whole for a minute before we consider the individual classes. The major portion of total costs is demand-related. The next largest portion is energy-related, and the smallest portion is customer-related. As of 1970, demand-related costs were 67 percent of the total, energy-related costs were 20 percent of the total, and customer costs were the remainder, or 13 percent of the total. I have checked the 1972 costs, and they have not changed much from the 1970 values. I would expect for the year 1974 that the relative order from largest to smallest would remain the same. However, because of increased fuel costs the energy component will probably comprise a larger percentage of the total costs.

The illustrations for the individual classes will be based on the year 1970. The level of each of the rates would have to be increased by about $.02 per kilowatthour to make them appropriate for 1974 conditions. The relative level among the rates, which is important to my subject, would not be affected by the addition of $.02 to each rate. In the strictest sense, demand costs would be affected somewhat by rising fuel costs but not enough to be of importance here.

For residential customers, the major portion of the costs are demand costs, which are about 54 percent of the total. About 18 percent are energy costs, which are the truly variable costs. And the balance, or 28 percent, is customer costs, which are incurred regardless of whether the customer takes any service.

Now let's take a look at the small commercial customers. The small commercial class would be very similar to the residential class. Again the major portion of the costs is demand-related; 56 percent are demand-related, 18 percent are energy-related, and 27 percent are customer-related costs. So these two classes look very similar in the aggregate. Let's take a look at the large commercial class. In our case, there are industrial customers in this class also. This class could include customers from fairly small offices or workshops to huge office buildings and big factories. Here, demand is 70 percent of the total cost. Energy costs are 24 percent, while customer costs are down to 6 percent of total costs. Now, that has an important bearing on the structure of the rate. The residential apartment building class has a cost structure very similar to that of the large commercial class. Some 66 percent of the total costs are demand costs, 28 percent are energy costs, and about 6 percent are customer costs. Those are the distributions we start off with in making our rates cost-based. With this type of a structure, especially in the residential and small commercial class, the customer costs have a very important bearing on the design of the rate.

We need to know more than this, however, to tell how much to charge the various sized customers. So we've gone into a long testing program to determine customer characteristics to allow us to relate the demand portion of the costs to the customer characteristics. On a sampling basis, we now test all customers to determine their coincidence factors, diversity factors, load factors, demands, and their consumption. As a result of this analysis, we can determine what the relative shares of the demand costs are for various sizes of customers depending on the factors I have ennumerated, namely, the diversity, the load factors, and demands. Not all customers use their electrical appliances, electrical machinery, or lights at the same time. This creates diversity in the demand of customers on the electrical system. The sum of all the parts is greater than the whole. That is, the sum of individual customer's maximum demands for electricity is greater than the sum total of the demands at any given time on any given portion of the electrical system—except, of course, close to the customer's premises where the full demand will be reflected. Any given class of customers has typical load characteristics, and a given size of customer within a class will also have typical characteristics. From this knowledge, gained by testing and analysis, the proper share of demand responsibility can be assessed to the various classes and sizes of customers.

The resulting demand allocation for the residential rates shows that for a small customer, demand costs are about $.026 per kilowatthour. For a medium-sized customer, the demand costs are about the same, and for a large customer, it drops to $.01. On the basis of the customer test we've made, we've found that the diversity among the very large customers is greater because the type of customer is different. Partially this is because, by law, religious customers are included in the very large residential customer group. Now, what type of a residential rate structure does this lead to? The energy costs are spread across the board equally to each kilowatthour of use. The customer costs really should be collected in one service charge, or if possible, in a minimum charge. With that in mind, we could design a rate that had a terminal charge equal to $.01 per kilowatthour plus the energy cost. For the medium-sized customer, the indicated rate would be the terminal charge plus $.016. Now, on top of that there should be, to cover all the customer costs, a $3.50 minimum charge. That's the way the arithmetic works out. What I have come up with looks like a promotional rate, if we believe some of the current literature at this time. But it's really a cost-based rate. It just happens that the customers' characteristics are such that a decreasing-unit-charge form of rate with a large minimum charge is called for.

Let's go to the next one, the small commercial class, taking the same type of customer load characteristics into account. Again I will divide the class for convenience into small, medium, and large customers. The small customer's demand costs vary from $.016 to about $.03 per kilowatthour. The demand cost for the medium-size customer is about $.035, and for the large-sized customer it has decreased to $.024 per kilowatthour. Again, you can see what's going to happen. The indicated terminal charge would be $.024 per kilowatthour plus the energy cost. For the medium-sized customer, the indicated block rate would be the terminal charge plus $.011. The $.011 differential is the difference between $.035 and $.024. The smaller demand costs of the smaller customer are overwhelmed by the customer costs. Since customer costs are some 28 percent of the total costs for this class, the minimum charge is again an important element. The indicated rate would look very much like the residential rate but with a $4.00 minimum charge to cover the customer costs in this class. This analysis leads, again, to what looks like a promotional rate.

Now, just to take it one step further, let's go to the large commercial rate and see where we end up. Because of the extreme spread in size, this class was separated into customer test groups that numbered about six. The demand costs for the smallest to the very largest customers are about as follows: for the smallest customers about $6.40 per kilowatthour, of maximum demand, and going on up in steps to the largest, $7.40, $7.70, $8.40, $8.50, and, presently, $8.60 for the largest. Here you've got what looks like a classic case for inverted rates. However, the consumption of the customers with demand costs under $8.40 is quite small compared to the use of those with demand costs of $8.40 or more. Remember that customer costs are only about 6 percent of the total costs for the class. Customer costs can be absorbed in the differences between $8.60 and the various other demand

58

Table 4-1
Indicated Block Charges (Assuming $.006 per Kilowatthour Energy Cost)

Range of Use	Residential Class	Small Commercial Class
Minimum-use range	$3.50 per month	$4.00 per month
Medium-use range	$.032 per Kwh	$.041 per Kwh
Large-use range	$.016 per Kwh	$.030 per Kwh
	Large Commercial Class	
All-use ranges	$8.60 per Kw per month, $.60 per Kwh	
	Apartment Building Class	
Small-use range	$8.90 per Kw per month, $.009 per Kwh	
Medium-use range	$8.40 per Kw per month, $.006 per Kwh	
Large-use range	$7.20 per Kw per month, $.006 per Kwh	

costs. As a matter of fact, the entire customer costs are just about equal to these differentials. The indicated rate for the large commercial class, therefore, is a flat energy and flat demand charge.

The last illustration is for the residential apartment building class. The small customer in this class has a demand cost of $8.90 per kilowatthour of maximum demand. The demand cost for the medium-sized customer is $8.40, while it is $7.20 for the largest. Since in the residential apartment class only about 6 percent of the total cost is customer-related, it does not require a large minimum charge. The customer costs can be taken care of by a $.003 step in the energy charge. Given the decreasing demand costs and the relatively small customer costs, you would expect the demand and energy rates to be declining block rates—and that's the way it does come out. The indicated charges for the terminal rates are a demand charge of $7.24 per kilowatthour of maximum demand and an energy rate large enough to cover the energy costs. For the medium-sized customer, the demand charge would be $8.42, and the energy charge would be the same as for the large customer. For the small customer, the demand charge would be $8.92, and the energy charge would be increased by $.003 per kilowatthour to cover the customer cost.

For your convenience I've tabulated the resulting rate forms (see Table 4-1). They are cost-based rates. I'll let you judge for yourself whether they also look promotional.

Notes

1. J. H. K. Shannahan quoted in *Public Utilities Fortnightly,* September 10, 1970, pp. 43-45.

2. Ibid.

3. Commissioner Carver of the Federal Power Commission quoted in *Public Utilities Fortnightly*, October 9, 1970, p. 42.

4. *Public Utilities Fortnightly*, June 10, 1971, pp. 92, 93.

5. Ibid.

5

Federal Financing of Electric Utilities in the Wake of Con Ed

William G. Rosenberg

In September 1973, I proposed a program which would modify the financing of the capital expansion of electric utilities. The proposal would provide a program of federal insurance and guarantees which would significantly reduce the cost of capital, and therefore the rates, in producing electricity.

Two major events have occurred since September 1973 which have accelerated the financial pressures on electric utilities and consumer resistance to utility rate increases and which have increased the attractiveness of my proposal. In November 1973 the energy crisis came to a head, and on April 23, 1974, Con Ed omitted a dividend, which has shaken the confidence of utility investors to the core.

Then, as now, innovative, aggressive, and equitable action is necessary if the public, the regulators, and the utilities are to deal with the tremendous conflicting pressures we face today.

On one side, we are faced with an ever-rising number of requests from utility companies for ever-increasing amounts of rate increases. There is no question that most of these applications are precipitated by financial pressures on the utilities caused by the public's increasing demand for electricity, the inflationary conditions in our country, and the dramatic increase in fuel costs.

On the other side, consumers have dramatically and consistently opposed utility rate increases in the face of their own general frustrations with inflation and the economy. The Public Service Commission has before it a clear direction from Governor Milliken's Special Commission on Energy, chaired by Prof. Paul McCracken of the University of Michigan:

A proper balance must be found between protection of consumers and the approval of rates that are substantial enough to maintain the financial integrity of the companies. Without the latter, earnings of these companies would be inadequate to raise the capital needed to assure meeting future energy needs of Michigan consumers and businesses, and preserve job opportunities in the state. The citizens of Michigan have a stake in the maintenance of healthy financial conditions for their public utilities, without which future service will not be assured.

With this in mind, the question becomes: What changes are needed to creatively cope with this conflict?

The recent actions of the Commission make it abundantly clear that it does not believe that the traditional approaches are adequate to solve this basic dilemma. The Commission has realized that regulation in the public interest involves being more than a passive, silent partner to the utilities, acquiescing in company decisions after the fact.

The Commission has ordered both Detroit Edison and Consumers Power to work with the Commission's staff in developing management objectives and realistic standards for measuring the attainment of these objectives.

The Commission has also ordered a performance audit of a construction project, the first such activity in the nation. Stanford Research Institute has been retained to review all the management decisions regarding the development and construction of the Consumers Power's Marysville Synthetic Natural Gas Plant. This plant, which accounts for 20 percent of the gas supply of Consumers Power, is presently producing gas at $2.65 per Mcf, which is raising the price of gas by 35 percent across the board to all customers.

The Commission has instituted flat-rate pricing for residential electric service, which in effect eliminates quantity discounts, which are unfair, uneconomic, and wasteful. In addition, we have developed and vigorously supported a home insulation program as part of gas service, to conserve natural gas.

The Public Service Commission, in its recent decisions, has strived to innovatively, aggressively, and fairly exercise its role as the purchasing agent for consumers, to guarantee that they are getting a good buy, and to assure that the long-term supply of utility service will be adequate. Recent events might indicate that we may not have gone far enough to assure investor confidence in Michigan's utilities, and the Commission will continue to do what is economically justified, whether such course is the most popular or acceptable to politicians on the campaign trail.

However, it is not the responsibility of Michigan, nor of any one state, to shoulder the entire burden of the electric utility industry. The problems of the industry are generic and national in scope. The Commission, the industry, and the consumers must seek relief beyond the limited confines of state agency hearing rooms. One such area for national action lies in the area of financing, which currently accounts for at least 30 percent of the cost of electric energy. The availability of capital at reasonable prices is central to the provision of an adequate supply of power to meet the needs of the consumer and of the economy.

I have proposed a program which I believe to be innovative, aggressive, and fair. I urge you to give serious consideration to this proposal as one equitable method of alleviating one of the major problems faced by regulators, the industry, and consumers.

The proposal is:

Innovative because it involves a new method of financing the ever-increasing and expensive capital expansion need of electric utilities

Aggressive because it demonstrates the type of thinking that must be undertaken in an attempt to solve the basic dilemma which we face

Fair because all those affected by the regulatory process will benefit

I am proposing, for your consideration, a program which would modify the methods of financing the capital expansion of electric utilities over the next several years. The proposal, which is being translated into bill form by Lee White, former chairperson of the Federal Power Commission, will be presented to Michigan Senators Griffin and Hart for introduction to Congress. It would provide a program of federal insurance and guarantees of utility debt for the purpose of assuring a smooth flow of capital to the hard-pressed electric industry, reduce the costs of capital—and therefore ameliorate the severe financial conditions of today—and subsequently reduce the monthly utility bill paid by the customer.

In placing the basic dilemma to which I referred in a broader perspective, we must measure, in some objective way, the financial pressures facing the electric utilities. I think we can do that, and I would point to three major factors.

First, there can be no doubt that when the financial facts are considered objectively, financial stress upon the companies is serious. The aftershocks of the decision of the board of directors of New York's Consolidated Edison are still reverberating through the industry. The actions of the board in deferring the three-hundred eighty-fourth dividend payment marked the end of an era when the financial stability of the electric utility industry was unquestioned.

The major result of the Con Ed action has been a fundamental and major loss of investor confidence in electric utilities. Investors have realized that electric utilities are no longer riskless, stable investments which will always pay reasonable dividends.

As the loss of confidence results in falling stock prices and higher bond interest yields, the cost of money to the companies increases. There is also a secondary effect. As the financial condition of the companies worsens, their bonds are down-rated by the major listing services. Down-rating leads to still higher interest costs and a further weakened financial structure. It is also leading to a practical inability to raise capital to meet existing construction programs, at least in the short term.

Without getting into great detail, it is becoming apparent that the current financial system for some utilities won't work. The capital system of these capital-intensive companies is in danger of falling of its own weight. Outstanding bond indentures, dating from the 1930s and 1940s, require that the issuance of new bonds be accompanied by the sale of additional common stock. However, with some stocks selling 30 or 40 percent below book value, new equity financing would cause a serious dilution of earnings per share. Where earnings per share have already declined to the dividend level, any further dilution resulting from the sale of equity means that the company cannot earn its dividend. Failure to pay the dividend spells financial disaster.

This is what happened to Con Ed. As a result, in a first step in bailing out the company, the New York Legislature has agreed to finance the $800 million cost of two new Con Ed generating plants.

Because of the financial repercussions from Con Ed, Detroit Edison and Consumers Power have postponed bond and stock sales and deferred construction programs. Last week, Detroit Edison sold a scaled-down bond issue at 10 percent, an historic high for the company.

Based on information available to the management and boards of the two companies, Detroit Edison announced on May 22, 1974 that it is postponing work on virtually all its construction program. This decision comes three weeks after a similar decision by Consumers Power to postpone construction of two nuclear plants and one fossil-fuel plant.

The Detroit Edison decision alone affects 8,028 Megawatts of electrical generating capacity, or an amount equivalent to that used by 1.3 million homes. The Consumers Power decision affects 3,450 Megawatts of electrical power—enough electricity for more than two cities the size of Detroit.

As a result of these decisions, there is a real possibility of brown-outs in Michigan in the future. This is particularly critical because Detroit Edison has decided to operate with less reserve capacity—15 instead of 20 percent—to meet peak demands. Each of Detroit Edison's four Monroe plants accounts for 10 percent of their system capability. Since the plants are large and new and involve untested technology of scale, an equipment failure in one or more of the plants could result in brown-outs or black-outs even this summer.

Consumers Power has also had its Palisades Nuclear Plant down since August 1973, and there is no assurance that it will be operating by the summer of 1974. The plant accounts for 15 percent of its electric system generating capacity. Any additional plant failures or fuel shortages brought on by an impending coal strike or a reimposition of the Arab oil embargo would create serious problems for Michigan.

These postponements in new plant construction, in my judgment, are directly related to the impact of Con Ed on the financial markets and the serious erosion of earnings resulting from higher fuel costs and reduced automotive industry activities brought on by the national economic picture and the energy crisis.

Second, in recent years, when there has been a decided decline in the attractiveness of utility securities, there is also a growing demand for electricity. The annual growth in demand for electricity, as projected last summer by the Edison Electric Institute, will almost double every 10 years through 1990, and new capacity will be several times as expensive as existing capacity. Overall demand was expected to grow at a rate of 6.3 percent in Michigan in the next 5 years. However, the changed prices of energy and unpredictable consequences of rampant inflation in our economy have put these projections into serious question. New load forecasts and construction forecasts are urgently needed as we face up to the problem of protecting the ability of public utilities to provide adequate service.

As a result of Con Ed, Argus Research Corporation, a national financial analysis firm, points out that some utilities "bear close watching since their ability to maintain their dividends is less certain." Among these "weak sisters" are Detroit Edison and Consumers Power. Both stocks were selling at 37 percent below book value as of May 24, 1974. These two companies supply about 80 percent of Michigan's electric power.

It is clear that the combination of growing demand for service, the energy crisis, and inflation is seriously eroding the attractiveness of utility securities. Unless there are some fundamental structural changes in the financial ground rules, investor-owned utilities will continue to file a steady stream of major rate increase applications, and some like Con Ed and perhaps other big-city utilities may simply run out of steam.

Third, the capital situation is even more dramatic when one considers that electric utilities face severe and increasing competition in the capital markets from the petroleum industry and others. It is anticipated that over the next 15 years, the worldwide petroleum industry will require $1 trillion in new funds, of which $400 billion must be raised from external sources—a 70 percent increase in annual capital investment over the 1971 level.

Public and consumer opposition to rate requests has dramatically increased. Recent calls for the resignation of various members of the Commission, threats of removal by political candidates, organized demonstration, and a wholesale consumer revolt in New York City are sure signs that consumers are angry.

Double-digit inflation has exerted enormous pressure on all consumers, as has unemployment, which in Michigan is twice the national average. With purchasing power rapidly fading, resentment at price increases set by public bodies, such as the Commission, is becoming vehement. Active intervention by consumer and environmental groups, unions, industrial companies, and local governmental units in rate proceedings has increased.

Clearly, a status quo, business-as-usual approach will only lead to disaster for the utilities and the public. We must come forward with the necessary innovations to meet the new problems.

It is within the economic and social perspectives which I have outlined, and in response to the mandate for sound regulation, that I have proposed a program of federal insurance and guarantee which, in my opinion, will significantly reduce capital cost and assure its availability to meet future demand for electricity.

A company's cost of capital is the composite of interest on long-term debt, return on preferred stock, and earnings on common stock. In 1971, total capital expenses amounted to 40 percent of the gross revenues of the electric utilities, and the cost of capital alone accounted for 30 percent. Thus it is clear that any reduction in cost of capital would create significant savings to the consumer.

My proposal would operate to reduce the cost of capital by lowering the interest rate of federally guaranteed utility bonds and by allowing a company to use more debt and less equity in its capital structure. Briefly, the mechanics of the program would operate in the following manner.

1. At the existing securities hearing, the electric utility would petition the state regulatory commission for authorization to issue debt securities to finance new construction and associated facilities or refinance debt.

2. After feasibility analysis, the Commission would certify that the proposal was in the public interest, that the money was proposed for the needed plant, well designed as to technology and fuels, and reasonably priced.

3. The electric utility would apply to the appropriate federal agency for federal insurance and guarantee of the proposed debt issue.

4. The federal agency, relying on state commission certification, would guarantee the debt service payments and would charge the utility an insurance fee sufficient to fund the risk of default.

5. The utility company would then make its usual public offering or private placement of its bonds, and the new facilities would be constructed under commission surveillance.

6. Debt service payments and the insurance fee would be made by the electric utility in accordance with the terms of the bond indenture.

7. In the event of default, debt service could be paid from the insurance pool or, if this pool were insufficient, from the U.S. Treasury.

This approach should result in significant savings in two areas: lower interest rates and greater leverage. With respect to interest rates, on the basis of 1972 data, I calculate that a differential of approximately 150 basis points could exist between interest rates on federally guaranteed utility bonds and conventional A-rated utility bonds. On May 22, 1974, Detroit Edison's A-rated bonds were selling at 10 percent, and 25-year treasury bonds were quoted at 8.06 percent.

The most significant savings under the proposal will, however, come from higher leverage resulting from use of a greater percentage of debt in the capital structure. Common equity, taking into account associated income taxes, is over 3 times more expensive than debt. Under the proposal of 80 percent debt and 20 percent equity for incremental investment, very little, if any, external equity must be raised because retained earnings should cover the lower equity requirement. Common stock issues are also the least reliable source of capital during times of uncertain risks.

Under conventional financing there is an optimal percentage of debt in the capital structure, which is dictated by the financial theory that as debt increases in percentage, both the cost of debt and the cost of equity rise as the risk to enterprise increases. However, with a federal guarantee, the percentage of debt should not affect the interest rate on the bonds since the underlying credit would be that of the U.S. Treasury.

In a nutshell, the proposal allows for cheaper debt and more of it. In concept, it would give to consumers of electricity similar benefits to those received by homeowners from the F.H.A.—to wit: available financing, higher leverage, lower and more stable interest rates. Although a determination of the precise magnitude of the savings in capital costs and the proportion of debt that becomes optimum is a matter of debate, I project a minimum of a 25 percent savings on new capital costs.

Further, the cost advantages of my proposal over conventional financing multiply if future equity costs are projected to occur, because the return on existing as well as future equity must be increased to these higher future levels.

Under the assumptions fully discussed in the detailed paper which I have made available, and based on 1972 conditions, I calculate that if the $80 billion in new construction and refinancing were financed under this proposal, the savings in capital costs would be approximately $2.1 billion per year after 1977 and $63 billion over the 30-year life of the bonds. Under the ratemaking process, this $63 billion of savings would be passed on to the consumer. In Michigan, the savings would be $5 billion over a 30-year period, amounting to $167 million per year over the life of the bonds.

There is ample precedent for providing federal financial assistance to energy companies and for federal guarantees of private debt. Tax credits, investment credits, and depletion allowances amounting to over $6 billion per year are examples of assistance to energy companies. Some of these tax subsidies are being replaced with an administered price structure that has turned out to be even more profitable to the oil and gas industry. The Rural Electrical Coop Electric and Telephone systems have been built with government financing from the beginning; and low-cost federal financing and guarantees for agriculture, shipping, small business, defense, housing, and international investment are examples of federal guarantees of private debt. Significantly, a high percentage of the loans made by the Export-Import Bank are for the financing of electric and other energy projects—but in such places as Algeria, Russia, and Japan.

Low-cost federal financing has been arranged for the liquefied natural gas plants in Algeria and is being contemplated for the natural gas purchases from Russia. In addition, Japan has received hundreds of millions of U.S. federal loans to finance the purchase of nuclear power plants and fuel. Toyota cars are being produced with electricity subsidized by the U.S. government, but Chevrolets produced in Flint must bear the full unsubsidized cost.

In these times of our nation's energy crisis, inflation, imbalance of payments, and utility problems, the government should provide the same financial assistance to Con Edison in New York, Detroit Edison in Michigan, Commonwealth Edison in Illinois, and Southern California Edison in California, as it gives to the Russians, Arabs, and Japanese.

To enact this program, it would be necessary for Congress to pass enabling legislation.

In closing, I would ask only that this analysis be conducted on the merits of the proposal—pragmatically and not politically or ideologically. There will be some who reject it out of hand by relating it to the public power versus private power struggles of the past. But the provision of electricity at reasonable rates is too important to be hampered by shopworn concepts and an unwillingness to consider needed innovation.

Federal insurance and guarantee would not replace private ownership and control, but, on the contrary, would enable the investor-owned electric utilities to finance their new construction at the lowest possible costs and would keep them viable in these difficult times. Current debt-equity ratios, coverage requirements, and indenture restrictions were developed in response to the problems of the depression and the utility holding company scandals of the 1930s, before new technology, environmental concerns, inflation, and the energy crisis of the 1970s became reality. The electric utilities, financial and academic communities, consumer groups, regulatory groups, regulatory commissions, and the federal government must take a hard, second look, if the electric utilities are to service the energy requirements of the coming decade.

6

Administrative Reform and the Regulatory Processes

Asher H. Ende

We keep hearing repeatedly and insistently that we are living in a world in which rapid, almost revolutionary change is the order of the day. Usually when people refer to this type of change, they have in mind changes in our social mores and patterns of behavior, as well as changes in our physical surroundings.

We are warned even by the most conservative pundits that we must accommodate and adapt to such changes, or else our society will be fragmented or destroyed. In fact, some of the more radical and impatient prognostics sadly advise us that it is already too late and that only basic revolution involving the destruction of the existing social order is available to us.

One area in which a radical and basic revolution with almost unforeseeable future portent and impact has been taking place is in the field of telecommunications. Did you ever stop to think that in a period of scarcely 100 years the various forms of electronic telecommunications have transformed our society from a series of distinct and separate enclaves into what may be truly called a global village? Until the end of the 1840s the transfer of intelligence over distance had scarcely changed in 5,000 years. Over that entire period, humans, for the most part, carried information with them. Thus, the speed of the transfer of communications depended on the speed of transportation. In other words, communications were carried by messenger, by runner, on horseback, by stagecoach, or by ships at sea. At best, it could traverse a few hundred miles a day, and usually much less than that. It is true that some attempts, like sending information by smoke signals during the day or by fires at night or by mirrors reflecting the sun, had been successful. These were, however, relatively few and haphazard and very slow in transmission. The one attempt which promised some measure of success was the use of semaphore signals from hilltop to hilltop, to be repeated on a line-of-sight basis. This method, however, also depended on sunlight or clear weather and the availability of unobstructed views over considerable distances.

The coming of telegraphy in the 1840s provided us with an instrument of monumental change. As the first telegraph wires spread across the land and cables were laid at the bottom of the oceans, for the first time distance disappeared as a barrier to the speedy exchange of intelligence between people in widely separated locations. No longer could the battle of New Orleans be fought weeks after the Treaty of Ghent was signed.

This change also required people to modify and adapt their social institutions. Originally telegraph messages, just as all other items in international commerce, were stopped at national borders and retransmitted in the neighboring country. For example, at the boundry between France and the German State of Grand Duchy of Baden, there was a telegraph office building straddling two sides of the frontier. Telegrams from France to Germany terminated on the French side of the building, were laboriously written out in French, translated to German, and then handed through a window to the German operator, who put them on the telegraph to their German destination.[1] Obviously, people could not long tolerate this type of artificial delay, and agreements were soon concluded for the through transmission of electronic signals across borders. To accommodate this, it became necessary to establish international agreements and then international institutions.[2] By 1865, scarcely 20 years after the invention of the telegraph, the first meeting of the International Telegraph Union took place. It is interesting to note that this organization, concerned with the transmission of intelligence, is the oldest surviving international organization still in operation today.[3]

Telegraphy was followed in the mid-1870s by the invention of telephony. Now people could not only exchange thoughts by means of electronic circuits, but could also actually speak to a recognizable voice at the other end of the telephone. Thus, before the turn of the last century, individuals could engage in business and social transactions and governments could exchange views promptly, if not instantaneously.

In the postwar era, matters have moved even more rapidly. Domestically the coaxial cable and microwave facilities and internationally the repeater cable and satellites have literally transformed communications and made them vital business and social necessities. The wave guide, laser, and fiber optics promise even greater future developments.

Within the last 50 years, the development of broadcasting, first for radio and then for television transmission, has brought the entire world into everyone's home. These two developments, and particularly television, have had a tremendous impact. Major events are no longer foreign things to be heard about long after they occurred; rather they are living, vibrant occurrences which we witness as they take place. An earthquake is not a history. Its havoc is an indelible picture on the mind. War is not a glorious adventure, but torn bodies and sobbing, fatherless children.

Television has had another important and often overlooked impact. The constraints of time and programming, as well as the span of attention, require that in a television program the issue or problem be stated, that it be developed and brought to a climax, and finally that it be resolved. All this is done within a period of 30 minutes or 1 hour. Even a super deluxe special program rarely allows more than 90 minutes to 2 hours from introduction to denouement. Solutions tend to be simplistic, often accompanied by or brought about by resorting to violence. Small wonder, then, that a generation brought up with more hours before the picture tube than in class or in church is impatient and expects prompt, if not instant, solutions and feels fully justified in resorting to the violence it has witnessed if the solutions it wants are delayed or denied.

The above-described general philosophy, or perhaps "attitude" is a better word, has spilled over into even the more placid world of academia and the consulting fraternity in the criticism of regulatory agencies. One hears, not only with increasing frequency but in voices and articles that carry a note of impatience and petulance, that the regulatory agencies have either outlived their day or should be radically altered or should be made a minor part of the major executive departments.[4] If one were to reflect, one might find this to be a particular form of ironic development. What was held only a few decades ago[5] as a flowering of an American political genius and as a method of safeguarding the public interest through the creation of a fourth arm of government has now become a bureaucratic impediment in an age when rapid change is not only the order of the day, but, apparently, the goal of the day. In fact, I might note as an aside that this conference on public utility regulation which I am addressing reflects the current mood. Our opening session has the "interesting" title "Can Regulation Curb Corporate Power?" Note that the subject is not "How Should Regulation Be Used to Curb Corporate Power?" Note that the subject is not "Should Regulation Be Used to Curb Corporate Power?" Note that the subject is not "Is Regulation Unduly Interfering with Corporate Initiative?" It is none of these, but rather starts out with an almost implicit assumption of the powerlessness or corruption of the current governmental structure.

As a former regulator, whose horns may yet be visible, I must confess that I have a strong, adverse visceral reaction whenever I encounter dogmatic attacks upon or denigration of the regulatory processes. Let me stress that I am referring to the system itself—that is, public responsibility for the manner in which activities vital to the public interest are conducted—and not any particular action, ruling, or proceeding of a regulatory agency. I believe that the concept of regulation is as sound today as it ever was and probably much more important in our highly mechanized and integrated society than ever before. What must be changed, and changed promptly and decisively, is the method by which we regulate and the perspectives we use in carrying out the regulation. In other words, the basic concept is not only sound, but more necessary than ever before. How it is executed must be changed to cope with today's problems and not to address yesterday's evils. The industries affected by public interest play an increasingly important role in our lives. Certainly the telephone, television, and other means of communication bulk far larger in our business and social affairs than a quarter century ago.

As a nation, we are no longer self-sufficient, and we must import much of what we use. As an urbanized society, we could not exist without a rapid, continuous flow of industrial goods out of the cities and of raw materials, as well as food, into the cities. As a world which has developed the atom bomb and the intercontinental ballistic missile, we must have, for our very physical survival, instantaneous telecommunications and other electronic devices designed to detect potential hostile action within seconds after it becomes a reality. Intelligent, forward-looking, and responsible regulation is, therefore, in my view, even more vital today than ever before. Regulation must be transformed so that it may address today's problems promptly, efficiently, and effectively. It must be enhanced in its competence to recognize, analyze, and cope with these problems. Finally, it must be staffed with people who have breadth of vision and technical competence and are sufficient in numbers to discharge the altered and enhanced role which, as I will discuss, must be entrusted to regulation.

Now, in any given society where large accumulations of capital are required or where the facts of life limit duplication simply because it is too costly and too inefficient, we must find means of controlling the agglomerations and accumulations of capital or power. There are various ways of doing that. Of course, one of those might, in the long run, be the enlightened self-interest of the persons who are running these large corporate entities. Unfortunately, people at this stage of their existence are not sufficiently aware that enlightened self-interest would, over the long run, prove the best of all approaches. We have, therefore, found it necessary to devise social controls to ensure that entities to which we grant monopolies or quasi-monopolies will act more or less in the public interest.

What are these social controls? In our society they are first the antitrust laws—to prevent monopoly, to provide for diversity, and to encourage competition in price, quality, and innovation. Unfortunately, these are not perfect instruments and are essentially negative in nature. They prohibit the bad—i.e., monopoly—in hope that this will result in the good—i.e., competition. Also, because they require lengthy investigation to prove a civil or criminal case which is judicial in nature, they are ponderous and slow-moving.

The second tool is called "regulation." It is available in a much narrower arena than the antitrust tool. It can be applied only where an industry or activity is so affected by the public interest as to warrant governmental control over entry and prices, as well as to ensure against discrimination and dishonesty. Regulation was designed to operate more efficiently and effectively than competition. It can pinpoint specific problems or issues and cure them. It can pick and choose between affirmative remedies. Not only can it prohibit, but it can also command affirmative action. At least in theory, it should provide for prompt action and reaction unhampered by ponderous procedures. In short, it should be a flexible multipurpose tool designed to meet specific problems, as well as to resolve basic policy issues.

While direct governmental regulation is not applicable to most industry, the antitrust laws do apply to all business activities, including those that are regulated.[6] Thus, in general, in dealing with regulated industry the responsible agency can, if it is in a position to make the proper findings,[7] use both the competition and the regulatory approach. But it, too, is indirect and time-consuming—hearings and rulemaking procedures can and do take years to conclude and may be appealed to the courts, causing further delays. The delays inherent in regulatory procedures are compounded by budgetary and staffing limitations. Thus, regulatory agencies are scarcely in a position to be fully effective in their dealings with all the entities subject to their jurisdiction, that is, AT&T, all the international carriers, as well as Comsat, Western Union, and the new specialized carriers.

At FCC these limitations were recognized many years ago, and necessary reliance was placed on another tool—competition. The Commission began to rely on competition as an aid and supplement to regulation as early as 1948 in the famous Three Circuits case where competing radio telegraph circuits were authorized.[8] The matter was litigated to the Supreme Court in the *FCC v. RCA*.[9] This resulted in a very clear ruling that even in this highly regulated field, if the Commission can warrant, as it were, that competition is reasonably feasible and will serve some public purpose, such as maintaining or improving service, the Commission, could, in fact, authorize competition.[10]

In the post-World War II period, when the electronics revolution opened up new and different potentials for using the electronic spectrum, the Federal Communications Commission supplemented its procompetition policy gradually. It licensed part of the newly available spectrum, to entities in various segments of industry for their private use.[11] Then a few years later, through the Carterfone decision,[12] the Commission opened up the peripheral attachment market; then in the MCI[13] and Specialized Carriers decisions,[14] the Commission opened up the interstate non-MTS market to competition. This was done on the theory that in those areas where investment requirements were not prohibitive and where there were no major economies of scale, competition should be permitted and even encouraged. In the domestic satellite field, where Congress had not imposed constraints, the Commission also authorized competitive entry.[15]

It is to be noted that in authorizing competition the Commission did not follow the precedent set with respect to other federally regulated activities, particularly transportation. In that field there is competition not only between various corporate entities, but also between different technologies, that is to say, that separate corporate entities operate the railroads, the buses, the truck lines, the barges, and the airplanes.[16] Thus in transportation, operating entities are not free to take advantage of the most efficient technologies available at any given time. In the communications field, with the single exception of international satellite communications where Comsat has been granted a statutory monopoly,[17] the Commission has followed the policy of allowing each entity to make use of all available technologies. Thus, all the carriers use, or have used, high-frequency radio, microwave, over the horizon scatter, wire lines, repeated cables, and coaxial cables. In the future, under this policy they will be free to use wave guides, lasers, and fiber optics, and, of course, at the present time several of the carriers are busily engaged in the construction of the satellite facilities to provide domestic communications service via satellite.[18] This policy may, in fact, at least partially account for the relative lack of serious problems in the case of most of the U.S. communication entities. They have been free to avail themselves of whatever technology was most promising to meet their particular service requirements and obligations.

The moves taken by the Commission to permit competition spurred AT&T into a series of countermoves designed to protect its position in the field and to meet the competitive threat posed by the Commission's policy determinations. In each instance it would appear that the AT&T reaction was designed to cope with the particular threat it visualized as resulting from the particular Commission actions. Thus, after the Commission adopted a policy which permitted noncarrier entities either individually or on a cooperative basis to make use of the microwave spectrum to meet their communication needs, AT&T revised its tariff filings to include a new category of pricing which it called "Telpak."[19] This tariff filing provided for very substantially reduced charges, depending upon the amount or quantum or capacity a customer might require. Hearings were instituted by the Commission to determine whether the charges for Telpak were just and reasonable and whether, in fact, Telpak was a new and different service.[20] At the cease of this hearing the Commission held that Telpak was, in essence, a charging technique rather than a new or different service, because services were provided over the identical facilities which had previously been used with only the charges made being different.[21] The Commission found that there was no justification whatever for two of the categories of Telpak originally offered, and the Commission reserved for future decision the question of the competitive necessity for two other categories.[22]

The Telpak proceeding plus other questions which arose from the Commission's rate case in Docket 16258[23] led the Commission into another series of hearings designed to determine a logical or rational basis upon which rates for different services provided over common facilities could be determined.[24] The concern of the Commission related, on the one hand, to the ensuring of the ability of the telephone company to compete fully and fairly with the new entities being licensed by the Commission, and, on the other hand, to be certain that the company was not improperly or discriminately fixing charges for certain categories or classifications of service and most particularly not cross-subsidizing its competitive services out of profits from its monopoly services, particularly the message telephone toll service. The proceedings designed to make these determinations were finally centralized in Docket 18128. The hearings in that proceeding have been closed; the proposed findings, conclusions, and other relevant documents have been filed by the parties, and the matter is now awaiting Commission decision.

As new and different services evolved, AT&T devised new and different tariff offerings. All these offerings were essentially designed to afford certain categories of customers who had reasonably large requirements, facilities, and services at rates which were less than what they would otherwise pay if they were charged a multiple of the basic, leased voice-grade service equal to the number of voice-grade services they required. Thus, AT&T made, on an experimental basis, a 50 kilobit offering[25] and a series 5000 offering,[26] and it filed a so-called hi-lo tariff[27] in which it proposed to charge different rates for leased circuits over higher-capacity facilities than those over low-capacity facilities. It also filed a relatively low-cost offering to take advantage of its ability to provide data under voice facilities over its existing microwave system.[28] Aside from the foregoing, AT&T also filed tariffs pursuant to which it made capacity available to so-called communication wholesalers, provided that those entities did not have long-distance facilities of their own.[29]

Most of these offerings have been attacked by the other carriers as unlawful and discriminatory and are now subject to hearings at one stage or another.[30]

The Commission's Carterfone decision, which was designed to permit entities to make use of nontelephone equipment provided such equipment was privately useful and not publicly harmful, has also stirred up major controversy. At first the Bell System indicated basic acceptance of the doctrine provided that adequate assurance could be given against harm to the system. The first step in providing such assurance was the introduction of a telephone company-supplied buffer between the equipment and the company lines.[31] Complaints soon arose about the cost of this buffer,[32] problems in getting the interconnection, and the limitations it placed on the ingenuity of other manufacturers. The Commission over the years has conducted a series of studies and inquiries, including one by the National

Science Foundation,[33] which were all designed to resolve the problems in a manner that would protect the integrity of the switched network and not hamper the ingenuity of independent manufacturers in providing more economic and useful attachments. Unfortunately, despite the many years of study and consultation, the issue has not been resolved. Instead, the telephone company has raised entirely new and different concerns. Essentially its basic argument is that if, in fact, these various attachments and substitutions of equipment are permitted, the telephone will necessarily lose substantial revenues. Since it is entitled to a fair rate of return, it will be required to increase charges for its other services to make up for this alleged loss in revenues. There have been all sorts and types of estimates made, including some running into many billions of dollars.[34]

Many state commissions, disturbed by what they felt to be an unwarranted federal encroachment into areas which has previously been the subject of their exclusive jurisdiction, have instituted various proceedings designed to limit the freedom and ability of users to attach such non-telephone company equipment as they think would be most useful to meet their needs. The growing controversy seems in many instances to have generated more heat than light and imposes the danger of a basic and probably unnecessary confrontation between the federal and state jurisdictions. It would appear clear that the telephone-switched network is a single nationwide facility capable of providing service via the identical facilities between telephones in neighboring states, in neighboring cities in the same state, in distant cities in different states, and to overseas and foreign points. This joint use has long been recognized and officially consecrated in various joint actions and decisions of the federal and state regulatory authorities. The investment and operating costs related to the plant are allocated between federal and state jurisdictions,[35] in accordance with separations procedures basically designed as a joint effort between the federal and state jurisdiction, although the federal jurisdiction has the ultimate power of prescription. At the present time, under the established separations procedures, something approximating 20 to 25 percent of the investment in and operating and maintenance cost of what is normally considered local exchange equipment, is actually assumed between federal jurisdiction and is paid for out of interstate charges and tolls.[36] In fact, the federal share of the investment and operating costs has been growing regularly over the years and promises to continue to grow.[37]

It must be recognized, of course, that there are specific problems which each of the states faces in its regulatory responsibilities and for which no particular individual course of action is necessarily optimum in all instances. It must also be recognized that the United States operates as an integrated economic unit and that the availability of efficient, low-cost communications services are vital to every aspect of American life—social, business, government, and national security. Under these circumstances any action which would look toward 50 separate enclaves, each operating under separate rules and regulations insofar as the facilities which may be available to users are concerned, is unthinkable; yet unthinkable though it may be, actions in several states tend to give rise to this potential. In response to this the Commission felt impelled to assert federal primacy while at the same time seeking the appropriate actions designed to take account of the legitimate concerns of the states.[38] The matter remains in litigation, with no easy solution in sight.

There is a further aspect to the changes caused by the introduction of competition. This relates to the reliance which the newly authorized carriers necessarily have to place on available facilities of AT&T to reach their customers. In essence, AT&T enjoys a monopoly in the local loop field, that is, the facilities connecting the customers' premises to the AT&T local exchange and that local exchange with the facilities of the new carriers. In addition, AT&T operates a nationwide network, and any part of the country can be reached through its facilities or the facilities of carriers with whom they interconnect. In order to compete effectively in the provision of their authorized services, the new and specialized carriers must rely on AT&T, particularly for the local loops.[39]

A whole series of problems have arisen with respect to the terms and conditions for interconnection, particularly the charges made. It has been alleged that AT&T has different charges for international specialized carriers from those imposed on its own long-lines department. Furthermore, it provides foreign exchange and other services to its own long-lines department, but allegedly refuses to provide similar facilities under the same terms and conditions to other carriers. These matters are also in study and litigation at the present time.[40]

In the last year AT&T has abandoned any pretense of being defensive with respect to the maintenance of its customers' services and facilities and has, instead, openly advocated a restoration of its monopoly position. In essence, it argues that in this field economies of scale are available; that the newly authorized competitors tend to serve the high-volume markets, thereby cream-skimming the field; and that the end result of the new competitive trend in regulation will necessarily be a multibillion dollar increase in the local-exchange telephone bills of the average nonbusiness user. The issue, then, has been joint in all aspects of the problem, that is, the basic philosophy, the pricing arena, and the ability to rely on the facilities of AT&T to complete the service patterns of the competing carriers.[41]

All the foregoing, rapid changes in demand, technology, and regulatory approach urgently require a review of the basic regulatory philosophy, particularly insofar as it relates to rates, charges, and the installation of facilities.

It is basically true that any new departure in government activity is usually triggered by a dramatic or traumatic event, or series of events, which clearly demonstrate the need for government intervention. This is, of course, particularly true with respect to the creation of the entire system of regulatory agencies in the early years of the Franklin D. Roosevelt administration. The country was in the throes of a serious depression —Congressional investigatory committees highlighted various practices which had grown up in the 1920s and which had seriously affected the various common carrier and utility services. The normal reaction of the Congress and of the administration was to propose enactment of legislation designed to cure the then-apparent evils and to prevent their recurrence. A large number of the evils related to financial transactions, pyramiding improper account-keeping and matters of that type. Accordingly, the Communications Act of 1934 was primarily designed to prevent fraud and to ensure honesty.

To meet the foregoing criteria, detailed systems of accounts were prescribed,[42] continuing property records were required,[43] interlocking directorates were prohibited, and officers and directors were barred from profiting from the negotiation of loans or the promotion of stock sales.[44] Detailed annual reports and other reports were required.[45] The regulatory agencies were given access to the accounts,[46] books, and records of the regulated entities, and in general a program of strict surveillance was prescribed and set up.

It is, therefore, not surprising that the basic thrust of the early years of regulation was toward the assurance of money honesty. Thus, great care was taken to ensure that every piece of equipment be recorded and that every record be backed up by a piece of equipment. Accounts were designed to ensure that every piece of equipment was recorded in an account at exactly the price paid for it. Depreciation accounting was designed usually on a straight life basis to ensure that the carrier did not recover more than was originally paid for the equipment less whatever was available at the end of its usefulness.

The return to be allowed to the carrier was normally fixed on the original investment, less depreciation. Thus, over the years it essentially became a cost-plus approach. This led to strong criticism that regulation was encouraging needless investment, because so long as the rate of return allowed to the carrier exceeded its cost of capital, the carrier would tend to maximize capital investment.[47]

Forty years of experience under the Communications Act demonstrates that the basic goals have, in fact, been achieved. Money honesty is really not a major issue. Generally speaking, records at the Commission show that except through inadvertence the carriers do not claim facilities which they have not purchased and installed. Furthermore, again, except through inadvertence, there is no indication that the carriers include in their books any property or costs other than those actually paid.

There is another consideration which must not be overlooked. In the past decade, there has been a virtual technological revolution which is still proceeding at an ever-accelerating pace. The electronic theory has been transformed almost beyond recognition. Change rather than stability is the order of the day. Technical obsolescence constantly occurs long before properties wear out physically. These changed factors, when coupled with the burgeoning demand and the ever-present inflation, require a reorientation in the entire approach to regulation. The basic issue now is not money honesty, but rather efficiency.

It is no longer a question of discovering whether the company did, in fact, install a particular piece of equipment. The question instead is, given present and reasonably foreseeable demand, what particular piece of equipment of all those available is best suited to meet such existing and potential demand. The question is not whether the price paid was properly recorded in the accounts. The question is rather, what checks were made to determine which available piece of equipment was most cost-effective from the point of view of original investment per usable unit, as well as to determine operating and maintenance costs. The question is not how sure are we that the particular piece of equipment will last for a maximum period of time, but rather, given current and foreseeable development in the technology, which piece of equipment is most cost-effective. The question is not how do we minimize annual depreciation charges. The question rather is, should we accelerate depreciation if that will allow us to recover costs more quickly and thereby support the installation of better, more economic equipment. In essence, the question is, can we develop reliable, maintenance-free, shorter-life plant at lower cost so that the physical and technical or economic lives will be closer to one another than is now the case.

The same questions as those just listed apply to operation and maintenance matters. The question is not do the books accurately reflect what the company actually paid for operations and maintenance. Instead, the question should be, how can the regulated carrier show that each claimed expenditure was, in fact, efficiently incurred and that each operation engaged in had, in fact, been conducted in the most cost-effective manner available. The question is not merely whether rates are just, reasonable, and equitable. The question rather is whether the rate levels, patterns, and structures are designed to encourage optimum and most efficient use of plant and to maximize savings and ensure the lowest possible rates to users.

Another major problem which confronts both the regulators and the carriers subject to their jurisdiction, as well as the public which requires services, is the delay between the time when a request or an action is initiated and the time that the final decision is made. Originally administrative agencies were created because it was felt that with less formality and greater expertise, these agencies would be able to act and react more promptly, efficiently, and knowledgeably than had been possible in the past through a combination of legislative enactment and judicial precedent. As the years went by, there was increasing concern with respect to alleged arbitrary actions on the part of administrative agencies.[48] As a result of these concerns, some of which were admittedly justified, the legislators have enacted an increasing number of provisions designed to ensure due process.[49] Unfortunately, due process necessarily involves delay. As a result of these legislative enactments, as well as increasing workloads and the natural bureaucratic encrustations which grow up through the years, the time lag between initiation and conclusion has become almost unbearably long.[50] It is a truism that justice delayed is justice denied. This truism is particularly applicable in the face of the current rapid technical changes, as well as ever-growing demand.

The above-described picture is a major factor in any consideration of how to enhance the efficiency and effectiveness of the entire system. A series of reform steps are necessary. First there is an urgent need for adequate support for the regulatory activity through the provision of essential budgetary allocations so that a competent staff which is sufficient in size to cope with existing problems and to plan ahead can be developed.[51]

The staffing necessary for regulatory agencies should put stress on procuring experts in the efficiency of regulated operations rather than experts who check into static compliance with rules. Thus, cost savings and rate-structure design which would enhance efficient use are more important than a detailed check of compliance to assure that particular items are in account A rather than account B, if, in fact, both accounts are either above-the-line accounts or below-the-line accounts. If stress on efficiency reduces total cost by an appreciable percentage and thus defers rate increases, in these days of inflation that is really the equivalent of a rate reduction. These savings in investment costs and in operating and maintenance costs are both in the short run and in the long run far more important to total user cost than the difference of some fraction of a percentage point in the allowed rate of return. In fact, the stress on efficiency and cost control would tend to be a countervailing force to the normal tendency to increase investment for rate-of-return regulation purposes. It would help restore a much healthier balance in the forces impinging upon executives of regulated utilities in their constant struggle to, on the one hand, provide the services the consumer needs, and to, on the other hand, satisfy the legitimate requirements of their stockholders who supply the capital essential to the installation and operation of the utility's plant.

To ensure efficiency, it is essential that all facets of regulatory agency activity be streamlined. Due process should not be equated with undue delay. Most important is the need to reexamine the various rules and regulations which call for ever-increasing volumes of paper, to cull out those items which serve no major useful purpose and to concentrate on those items which contain necessary and vital information. The system of accounts and records should be redesigned to emphasize the production of data which tests the efficiency of both the overall operation and each individual proposal rather than the honesty of the utility. Such honesty can be ensured by periodically unscheduled reviews and checks.

Application procedures and forms should be revised so that the carrier would be required to show, first, the need for the facility in question, second, the alternative available to satisfy that need, third, how the particular alternative chosen by the carrier satisfies the need and, most important, why that alternative is most efficient and cost-effective; and finally, that it should be demonstrated by the carrier that the particular item in the alternative chosen was purchased at the lowest available price either through competitive bidding or through other means that ensure that the price paid was the lowest available.

The current procedures whereby an application is unduly delayed because filing upon filing is permitted or required should be altered. General rules with respect to areas of service and types of facilities should be developed through notice of inquiry or rulemaking procedures. Once such rules have been devised, any application filed in accordance with the general rules should become automatically effective within a specified period not to exceed 60 days unless the Commission, by affirmative action and for reasons stated, defers that effective date. The carrier, in turn, should assume the risk that the item or activity which was authorized under this procedure would not be allowed as a claimed rate base or expense item, if a postaudit, no matter when conducted, discloses either that the carrier was guilty of a material misstatement or that the action was not in accordance with current rules.

Similar reforms are necessary with respect to rate cases. At the present time, rate proceedings have almost degenerated into a sort of ritualistic scenario. In essence, the major thrust of the proceeding relates to a determination of the cost of imbedded debt and theoretical debates between company and public witnesses about how the present and reasonably foreseeable cost equity should be determined under statutory standards. After these two items are resolved, the question of the appropriate capital structure is considered and then, on the basis of that determination, the rate of return is fixed by a mathematical formula.

In these current times of rampant inflation, rapid technical change, and continuing high demand, greater stress should be placed on the question of cost effectiveness and efficiency. What is the ideal capital structure in an era when high-quality bonds require interest approaching, if not exceeding, 10 percent and contain clauses against refinancing for a period from 5 to 10 years? In this era, are not cost control and efficient operation more important than any particular level of rate of return? Shouldn't the stress be on encouraging the regulated utility to concentrate more on reducing cost than on enhancing the particular numerical rate of return allowed by the carrier? Shouldn't the carrier be encouraged to stress efficiency by an indication that its performance would be judged on those criteria rather than on reaching or exceeding a particular mathematical ratio between after-tax profits and investment?

In sum, the entire outlook toward regulatory activity should be revised as follows:

1. By modifying the concept of natural economic monopoly in light of technological change.
2. By recognizing competition for what it is, that is, an important tool in ensuring efficiency and responsiveness to customer demand.
3. By taking care to prevent large, well-entrenched entities from using their current positions to compete unfairly either by cross-subsidization or by denial of access to facilities where they have a virtual monopoly.
4. By taking care to differentiate between allowing feasible competition and fragmenting of the industry between too many entities none of whom can obtain sufficient traffic to prosper. Since, by definition, regulated utilities and carriers provide an essential service, the administrative agencies must at all times assure themselves, first, that the necessary services will be continued; second, that there is sufficient traffic or business to support the competition they permit; and, third, that the new entrant makes a reasonable showing that this entry will result in some public benefit in the way of new, improved, or different services or lower charges.
5. By streamlining regulatory procedures to prevent delay.
6. By shifting the emphasis in regulatory procedures from checking on accuracy and honesty toward testing efficiency and economy.
7. By placing greater reliance upon, and providing for, quasi-automatic grants, upon demonstration that the rules have been complied with.
8. By encouraging and prescribing ratemaking designed to maximize efficient use of plant.
9. By revising depreciation procedures to reflect the current, rapid technical change and the potential economies available from keying plant to technical rather than physical life.

10. By instituting investigatory procedures which stress efficiency and economy of operation.
11. By moving toward greater examination into cost effectiveness of investment and efficiency of operation in rate-of-return proceedings.
12. By encouraging efficient operation through appropriate allowances for increased earnings due to efficiency rather than increased earnings due to higher rates.
13. By allowances of returns to carriers which reflect not only the foregoing, but also the effects of the current inflationary era on the ability to raise both debt and equity.
14. By allowance of returns to carriers which reflect the additional risks resulting from the introduction of competition.
15. Finally, by ensuring that the regulatory agency is adequately financed so that it may staff itself with the proper number of competent employees particularly skilled in testing efficiency, cost effectiveness, and responsiveness to technical change.

Notes

1. *From Semaphore to Satellite,* published by the International Telecommunications Union, Geneva, 1965, p. 45.

2. Ibid., pp. 45, 48, and 49.

3. Ibid., pp. 48, 63, and 65.

4. A new regulatory framework, *Report on Selected Independent Regulatory Agencies.* The President's Advisory Council on Executive Organization, Superintendent of Documents, U.S. Government Printing Office, January 1971, pp. 3-7. And *Reform Regulation,* an evaluation of the Ash Council Proposals, a staff paper by Roger G. Noll, the Brookings Institution, Washington, D.C. 1971, pp. 110-111.

5. *Report on Regulatory Agencies to the President Elect,* by John M. Landis, 1960.

6. Communications Act of 1934, as amended, 47 U.S. 313; *McLean Trucking Co. v. U.S.,* 320 U.S. 67.

7. *FCC v. RCA Communications, Inc.,* 346 U.S. 86, 96:

We therefore do not say that authorization of Mackay under all the relevant circumstances including the significance the Commission may rightly attribute to the facts on the basis of its experience may not be in the public interest.

8. Mackay Radio and Telegraph Co., Inc., 15 FCC 690.

9. *FCC v. RCA Communications, Inc.*, 346 U.S. 86.

10. Ibid.

11. In the Matter of the Allocation of Frequencies in Bands above 890 Mc., 29 FCC 825.

12. Carterfone, 13 FCC2d 420.

13. Microwave Communications, Inc., 13 FCC2d 953, 21 FCC2d 190.

14. Specialized Common Carriers Rulemaking, 29 FCC2d 870, 31 FCC2d 1106.

15. Domestic Satellite Rulemaking, 35 FCC2d 844.

16. Interstate Commerce Act, 49 U.S.C. 1 (Railroad and Pipeline Carriers); 49 U.S.C. 141 (Inland Waterway Transportation); 49 U.S.C. 301 (Motor Carriers); and 49 U.S.C. 401 (Civil Aeronautics).

17. Communications Satellite System, 47 U.S.C. 701.

18. Domestic Satellite Rulemaking, 35 FCC2d 844.

19. AT&T Tariff FCC No. 260, Series 5000, private line services.

20. Telpak 38 FCC 370, 374.

21. Ibid., p. 395.

22. Ibid.

23. AT&T 9 FCC2d 30, 9 FCC2d 960, 10 FCC2d 705, 11 FCC2d 84.

24. AT&T 13 FCC2d 853 and 18 FCC2d 761.

25. AT&T Tariff FCC No. 263.

26. AT&T Tariff FCC No. 260.

27. AT&T Tariff FCC No. 260, Series 2000 and 3000.

28. AT&T Tariff FCC No. 267.

29. AT&T Tariff FCC No. 260 and FCC 266.

30. AT&T 44 FCC2d 697 and 45 FCC2d 88.

31. AT&T Tariff FCC No. 263, regulation 2.6.

32. See comments and recommendations filed in connection with economic implications and interrelationships arising from policies and practices relative to customer interconnection (Docket No. 20034, 46 FCC2d 214) and correspondence filed relative to foregoing. Both documents are available at the offices of the Common Carrier Bureau of the Federal Communications Commission, 1919 M Street in Washington, D.C.

33. *A Technical Analysis of Common Carriers–User Interconnection*, National Academy of Sciences, June 1970.

34. Customer Interconnection et al., 46 FCC2d 214.

35. Communications Act of 1934, as amended, 47 U.S.C. 221(c).

36. Separations Procedures, 23 FCC2d 465, 25 FCC2d 123, 26 FCC2d 247.

37. Separations Procedures, 26 FCC2d 247, 260-261.

38. Telerent et al., 45 FCC2d 204. Appeal pending in U.S. Court of Appeals for the 5th Circuit; Customer Interconnection et al., 46 FCC2d 214.

39. Specialized Common Carrier Services, 29 FCC2d 870, 940.

40. Bell System Tariff Offerings, 46 FCC2d, 413, affirm sub non *Bell Telephone Company of Pennsylvania et al. v. FCC and U.S. of America* (3d CCA), September 11, 1974.

41. An Unusual Obligation, speech by Mr. John deButts, Chairman of the Board of AT&T before the National Association of Regulatory and Utility Commissioners, Seattle, Wash., October 1973.

42. Communications Act of 1934, as amended, 47 U.S.C. 220.

43. Ibid., 47 U.S.C. 213.

44. Ibid., 47 U.S.C. 212.

45. Ibid., 47 U.S.C. 219.

46. Ibid., 47 U.S.C. 220.

47. Behavior of Firm under Regulatory Constraint, Harvey Avrich and Leland L. Johnson, *American Economic Review,* December 1962, 52, 1053-1069.

48. Attorney General's Manual on the Administrative Procedure Act (1947).

49. Administrative Procedure and Judicial Review, 5 U.S.C. 551.

50. *The Report of Pending Applications and Hearing Cases Filed,* July 31, 1974, by the FCC with the Senate Commerce Committee lists 72 pages of pending matters more than 3 months old.

51. In 1963 the total Common Carrier Bureau staff was 149. In 1973 it was 170 plus 53 authorized positions for a Special Task Force conducting an in-depth investigation into AT&T.

7 Irreversibility of Pollution and Depreciation Policies

Barbara B. Murray

Concern with the pollution or the environmental problem is not a recent phenomenon. However, a new factor has been added—mainly the magnification of our ability to damage our environment, perhaps irreparably. The issue of the irreversibility of pollution cost or environmental damage is implicit in our statements of pollution abatement, pollution control, or environmental destruction. These terms imply some degree of risk of irreversible pollution damage to the environment. Our concern is not to completely control all forms and types of pollution, but rather to control them to the extent that the pollution has a substantial risk of damage and/or irreversibility.

The type of policy chosen to deal with pollution is a function of the degree of risk or irreversibility associated with the pollution. For those forms of pollution which have the greatest risk of irreversible damage, as death or permanent impairment, the policy option has been to prohibit the production of the particular form or type of pollution. At the other end of the scale are those forms of pollution which have a low risk of irreversibility. For this type of pollution, the policies proposed have been primarily variations on the emission-fee policy, or the pricing of the use of environmental resources. In the middle range of irreversibility are those forms of pollution which are felt to have a higher risk of irreversible damage, but which can be mitigated or neutralized by requiring investment in pollution equipment. In this type of situation, the policy option has been to require the installation of pollution abatement equipment.

These various types of policies were developed without perfect knowledge as to the degree or risk of irreversible pollution damage. We do not have satisfactory methods to measure the risk of irreversibility or the social cost associated with the different types and forms of pollution. Consequently, society has had to choose from among the various policy options—ranging from doing nothing to prohibition—that policy which best reflects the implicit degree or risk of irreversible pollution damage. In other words, society is trying to select a portfolio of policies to ensure minimum risk of irreversible pollution damage to the environment.

Investment and Depreciation of Pollution Equipment

Pollution equipment policies imply a larger risk of irreversible pollution damage than do emission-fee policies. Assuming that society does decide that the capital equipment policy is necessary for a particular type or form of pollution, there is the problem of choosing a depreciation policy to allocate the capital charges over time. Should there be an accelerated depreciation policy where current users pay a larger proportion of the capital charges? This assumes that current users should pay a larger proportion of the capital charges because the equipment was installed for their benefit. Or, it could be argued that current users should pay a larger proportion of the capital charges so as to reflect the cost of the irreversible pollution damage which they would have inflicted on future users if the equipment had not been installed.

Alternatively, should there be a decelerated depreciation policy where future users pay a larger proportion of the capital charges? This stance assumes that future users should compensate current users for the benefits of a cleaner environment, or that the equipment was installed primarily for the benefit of future users rather than current users.

In addition, the choice of a depreciation policy is to choose an intertemporal stream of prices that allows the recovery of a firm's initial investment in an asset. But, as William Baumol[1] also notes, the cost of the investment includes the cost of capital: ". . . it seems rational *from the point of view of society* that an investment be undertaken only if it is expected to offer at least this return. For if consumers of the goods or services to be produced with the aid of the investment are unwilling to pay in *real terms* the opportunity cost of obtaining the asset in question, then construction of the asset by definition represents a wasteful use of resources."[2]

Depreciation policies should also take into account *functional depreciation,* the depreciation that occurs when capital equipment is rendered obsolete by a new technology, is made inadequate by the growth in demand, or is made useless by changes in public policies. These aspects of functional depreciation—particularly changes in technology and public policies—are relevant for pollution equipment.

In Baumol's model he has developed a capital recovery depreciation model that does take into account technological change. The basic assumptions of his model are that capital is added in each period at a constant cost and that demand (or public policies for the purpose of our discussion in this chapter) changes so rapidly that the asset is used to capacity in the period in which it is installed, requiring a new asset in each succeeding period.

In applying these assumptions to pollution equipment investment, we can envision two types of situation. First, output is defined in terms of the reduction in possible irreversible pollution damage. If the risk of irreversibility increases so rapidly that the old equipment is used to capacity in the period in which it was installed, new pollution equipment would be needed in the succeeding period to meet the higher risk of irreversibility. Second, output can be defined in terms of quantity and quality variables. For example, output would be defined in terms of the amount of allowable pollution. If demand increased, due to factors other than changes in the risk of irreversible pollution damage or changes in public policies, the equipment would be used to capacity, and new pollution equipment would have to be installed to meet the increase in demand.

Capital Recovery and Present-value Depreciation Charges

The capital recovery depreciation method used by Baumol incorporates technological change by assuming that the replacement cost of the asset decreases by a *fixed* percentage in *each* period, by the rate of technological change (h). The cost of the asset in any period (t) is defined as

$$v_t = v_0(1 - h) \tag{7.1}$$

where v_0 = initial cost of the asset

h = rate of technological change

The capital recovery depreciation charges for any period (t) are determined as follows:

$$\mu_T = v_t \frac{r + h}{1 - \left(\dfrac{1 - h}{1 + r} \right)^n} \tag{7.2}$$

where μ_T = the current dollar or capital recovery depreciation charge

v_t = cost or present value of the asset in period (t)

n = life of the asset

r = discount rate which is equal to the cost of capital

Having determined the annual cash flows by Equation (7.2), we find that the present value of the asset at the end of any period (t) can be determined by

$$A_t = \sum_{j=t+1}^{n} \frac{\mu_j}{(1 + r)^j} \tag{7.3}$$

where μ_j = capital recovery depreciation charges

A_t = present value of the asset for period (t)

It is then possible to determine the present-value depreciation charge or the loss in economic value for any period (t) as

$$D_t = v_t - 1 - v_t \tag{7.4}$$

where D_t = the present value depreciation charge for period (t)

Examples of the Depreciation Schedules

By using the capital recovery formula and present-value formula, the two depreciation schedules are as indicated in Table 7-1, for an asset with an initial cost of $1,000, zero scrap value, a 5-year life, a discount rate of 6 percent, and various values of technological change (h).

If technological change is zero or not taken into account, the depreciation charges using the capital recovery method are constant over the life of the asset. In contrast, the present-value depreciation charges have an increasing, or decelerated, time pattern. This decelerated time pattern of present-value depreciation charges is similar to the results of Bruce Jaffee's[3] model, in which the objective of the regulated firm is to maximize its discounted cash flows.

When technological change is positive, the capital recovery depreciation charges have a decreasing, or accelerated, time pattern. As the rate of technological change becomes similar to the discount rate, or cost of capital, the present-value depreciation charges also have an accelerated, or decreasing, time pattern. It should be noted that for low values of h relative to r, the present-value depreciation charges will still have a decelerated time pattern. It is not until h becomes similar to r that these depreciation charges have an accelerated time pattern.

Also, when technological change is positive, the firm does not earn the cost of capital under either depreciation method. As indicated in Table 7-2, the effective internal rate of return is less than the discount rate or cost of capital.

Implications of the Different Depreciation Time Patterns

At low rates of technological change relative to the cost of capital, the present-value depreciation charges place a larger proportion of the capital charges on future users. This implies that future users receive a larger share of the benefits, in terms of receiving an environment with less irreversible pollution damage. Or alternatively, it implies that the pollution equipment investment was mandated by society for the benefit of future generations and that these users are paying for these benefits.

In contrast, the capital recovery method places the largest proportion of the capital charges on current users. This time pattern reflects the argument

Table 7-1
Current Dollar Depreciation (u) and Present-value Depreciation (v) Charges under Various Rates of Technological Change (h)

Original Cost = $1,000
Salvage Value = 0
Life = 5 years
Discount Rate = 6 percent

Period	$h = 0$		$h = 0.02$		$h = 0.06$		$h = 0.12$		$h = 0.14$		$h = 0.15$	
	u	v	u	v	u	v	u	v	u	v	u	v
1	$237	$178	$242	$190	$250	$214	$262	$251	$265	$264	$267	$270
2	237	188	237	194	235	206	230	222	228	227	226	230
3	237	199	232	199	221	200	203	197	196	196	192	195
4	237	211	227	205	207	193	178	174	168	168	164	165
5	237	224	223	212	195	188	158	155	145	145	139	140
Total depreciation charge	1,185	1,000	1,161	1,000	1,108	1,000	1,029	1,000	1,002	1,000	990	1,000

Table 7-2
Internal Rate of Return for Various Rates of Technological Change (h) and a Discount Rate of 6 Percent

h *(Percent)*	*Internal Rate of Return (Percent)*
0.5	5.84
1.5	5.48
2.0	5.20
3.0	4.90
6.0	3.80
12.0	1.20
14.0	0.12
15.0	−0.37

that we owe it to future generations to provide them with a clean environment. Another rationale would be that the risk of irreversible pollution damage was more immediate, and so large, that present users would have to install the equipment now rather than wait for a newer and less expensive technology. Under these circumstances, the investment is made for the benefit of current users, and they would pay a larger proportion of the capital charges for a soon-to-be-obsolete pollution equipment investment.

There are also some income redistribution aspects associated with the time pattern of depreciation charges. If future generations have higher real incomes than current users, assessing a larger proportion of the depreciation charges to current users redistributes income to future users. Also, by providing an environment with less irreversible pollution damage, present users are providing a redistribution of income in kind. To also place larger depreciation charges on present users would further redistribute income to future users. The use of a present-value or decelerated depreciation policy would reduce the intergenerational subsidy.

An Overview

The basic premise of this chapter is that the type of pollution policy chosen by society is a function of the degree of risk of irreversible pollution damage. Emission-fee policies are implicitly assuming a low risk of irreversibility, in that the environment has the ability to absorb or assimilate a finite amount of pollutants and/or that the pollution can be "cleaned up" at a later date. Other forms or types of pollution damage are considered to have such a high risk of irreversibility that they are prohibited, as, for example, the ban on DDT. Pollution equipment policies also imply a high risk of irreversibility associated with the pollutants, but their irreversibility can be "neutralized" with capital equipment investment. An example would be the proposed "scrubbers" for the electric power industry.

Given that society has chosen a pollution equipment policy for various forms and types of pollution which have a large risk of irreversible damage, there is the problem of deciding upon a depreciation policy. The choice of a depreciation policy is the selection of one of the many possible streams of intertemporal prices that reflect the loss in economic value of the asset and the benefits derived from the investment. The sum of the capital charges should cover the initial cost of the asset (which may be more or less than the replacement cost of the asset) and the cost of capital. These capital charges should also reflect for whom the investment was and to whom the benefits accrue.

Assuming that technological change is positive, but less than the discount rate, the capital recovery method of determining depreciation charges provides an accelerated, or decreasing, time pattern of charges. Current users pay a larger proportion of the capital charges than future users. This implies that the investment was made primarily for the benefit of current users. In contrast, the present-value method of determining depreciation charges has a decelerated, or increasing, time pattern of capital charges. The implication here is that the investment was made primarily for the benefit of future users.

If the investment in pollution equipment is undertaken primarily for the benefit of future users, the present-value depreciation method would assign the largest proportion of the capital charges to these users who receive the largest proportion of the benefits in terms of a less irreversibly damaged environment. Alternatively, if the investment is made to benefit current users or to assign the cost of possible irreversible damage, the largest proportion of the depreciation charges on current users would occur with the capital recovery method of depreciation.

When the rate of technological change is similar to the discount rate, both depreciation methods have an accelerated, or decreasing, time pattern of capital charges. The implication here is that because the risks of irreversible damage are so great and/or immediate, the investment is required even though a new technology is on the horizon. Current users are not willing to take the risk of waiting. The pollution equipment investment is made for their benefit, and either method would assign the largest proportion of the capital charges on current users.

As was previously noted, when technological change is positive, the effective internal rate of return is less than the discount rate. The depreciation charges would not cover the initial cost of the asset plus the cost of capital. If the discount rate were also to include the risk of irreversibility, the cost of capital could be recovered. This would not change the time pattern of the depreciation charges of either method; it would just increase the charges by an amount sufficient to cover the initial investment plus cost of capital.

We do not know the explicit risk of irreversibility of the various forms and types of pollution, or in many cases the rate and timing of technological change. It is this lack of perfect knowledge that has led to different positions with respect to public policy for pollution control. Those who estimate a higher risk of irreversibility would probably argue for prohibition or pollution equipment policies. They would argue that the risks were too great to wait for the new technology, or that the risks were greater than the rate of anticipated technological change. On the other hand, those who estimate low risks of irreversibility and high rates of technological change would probably argue for a "do nothing" policy or an emission-fee policy. But, if a pollution equipment investment policy is chosen in order to provide a cleaner, less damaged environment for future generations, a decelerated, or increasing, time pattern of depreciation charges would seem to be the most equitable. Alternatively, if the investment is made for the benefit of current users and/or so that current users should provide to future users an undamaged environment, an accelerated, or decreasing, time pattern of depreciation charges would be chosen.

This chapter has sought to bring attention to the importance of the risk of irreversibility as a variable in the selection of pollution policies. Certainly irreversibility affects the social costs and benefits of pollution. If all forms and types of pollution were reversible and technological change were rapid, society would probably not have as deep a concern with respect to pollution. It would probably be willing to wait for a new technology rather than impose policies based on the current technology. In addition, the long-run cost of "cleaning up" the pollution could be less because of the rapid rate of technological change. Just on the basis of the laws of diminishing returns and variable proportions, it would seem that irreversibility would bring about decreasing returns in production and increasing marginal utility for the reduction in irreversible pollution damage.

Notes

1. "Optimal Depreciation Policy: Pricing the Products of Durable Assets," William J. Baumol, *The Bell Journal of Economics and Management Science,* Autumn 1971, pp. 638-652.

2. Ibid., p. 642.

3. "Depreciation in a Simple Regulatory Model," Bruce Jaffee, *The Bell Journal of Economics and Management Science,* Spring 1973, pp. 228-342.

Index

Index

AT&T, 19, 73, 74, 75, 76
Adams, Walter, xiv
Administrative Reform, 69-85
Alberta & Southern Gas Company, Ltd., 34
Algeria, 68
Algonquin Gas Transmission, 29
Allied Chemical, 47
American Public Gas Association, 23, 32, 41, 51
American Public Power Association, 51
Amoco, 41
Arabs, 9, 64, 68
Arco, 45, 48
Argus Research Corporation, 65
Arkansas-Louisiana Gas Company, 28
artificial gas, xv
Atlantic Gas Light, 34
Atlantic Richfield Company, 48
Atlantic Seaboard, 25

Baltimore Gas and Electric Company, 28
Baumol, William, 88, 89, 94
BEDCO (Beneficial Exploration and Development Corporation, 34, 35
Belco Petroleum Corporation, 42-44
Bell System, 75
Bethlehem Steel, 28
Black & Decker Manufacturing Company, 28
Boulding, Kenneth E., xv, xvi
Brooklyn Union Gas Company, 34

California, 9
Capital Recovery, 89-90
Caterfone decision, 73, 75
Central Illinois Light Company, 36
Chevrolet, 68
Chicagoans, xiv
Cities Service Gas Company, 30, 44
Cleveland, Grover, 14
Columbia Gas Transmission Corporation, 28, 30
Commonwealth Edison in Illinois, 68
Communications Act of 1934, 78
Comsat, 73, 74
Consolidation Coal Company, 37
Consolidated Edison, xv, 16, 34, 61, 63-65, 68
Consolidated Gas Supply Corporation, 26
Continental Oil, 45, 47
Consumer Federation of America, 41, 51
Consumers Power Company, 35, 62, 64-65
Consumer Rates, 33-35
Curtailment Priorities, 27-28

DDT, 92
Depreciation Schedules, 90
Depreciation Time Patterns, 90-92
Detroit Edison, 10, 62, 64-66, 68

East India Company, 16
Edison Electric Institute, 65
El Paso Algeria, 28, 30
El Paso Natural Gas Company, 22, 25-26, 37
Elizabethtown Gas Company, 36
Ende, Asher, xiv
Energy Policy Project, 7
European Middle Ages, 4
Evolution, Law of, 2-3, 7-8
Exploration and Development Programs, 33-35
Export-Import Bank, 68
Exxon Corporation, 34, 45-47

FCC, 73
FPC Proceedings, 47-49
Federal Financing, 61-68
Federal Power Commission, xv, 21-51, 53, 61, 63
Federal Trade Commission, 47
Federalist Papers, 18, 20
Ford Foundation, 7-8
Forrester analysis, 6

Gary, Eldert H., 14-15
Gas Adjustment Clauses, 22-23
Gas Curtailment Report, 28
Getty, 45
W. R. Grace Company, 28, 47
Great Age of Change, 4
Griffin, Senator, 63

Hardin, Garret, 1
Hart, Senator, 63

ICC, 14, 15, 17
ITT v. General Telephone and Electric, 19
Ice Age, 6-7
Incremental Pricing, 23-25
India, 10
Inexco Oil Company, 34
Interlocking Relationships, 45-46
Interstate Commerce Act, 14
Irish, 10

Japan, 68
Justice Department, 47

97

List of Contributors

Kenneth E. Boulding is Director of the Program of Research on General Social and Economic Dynamics at the Institute of Behavioral Science, the University of Colorado. He is a past president of the American Economic Association, the Society for General Systems Research, the Peace Research Society, and the Association for the Study of the Grants Economy.

Walter Adams, ending his term as Michigan State University's thirteenth president, returned to the faculty as a distinguished university professor and professor of economics in 1970. A nationally known economist, Dr. Adams has been a consultant to the Senate Judiciary Committee and to the Small Business Committees of both houses of Congress. During the Eisenhower Administration, he served on the Attorney General's National Committee to Study the Antitrust Laws; during the Kennedy and Johnson Administrations, he served on the U.S. Advisory Commission on International Educational and Cultural Affairs.

David S. Schwartz is Assistant Chief of the Office of Economics for the Federal Power Commission. He has previously served the FPC in the positions of Public Utility Specialist, Senior Economist, and Chief of the Division of Economic Studies. Dr. Schwartz has frequently given expert testimony before various congressional committees and subcommittees.

John Monsees is a licensed professional engineer who has been employed by Consolidated Edison since 1947. He has served in the Rate Engineering Department as a staff analyst, associate manager, rate engineer, and, since 1970, its Director.

William G. Rosenberg is Chairman of the Michigan Public Service Commission and Executive Secretary to the Governor of Michigan's Special Commission on Energy. He has also served as Executive Director of the Michigan State Housing Development Authority.

Asher H. Ende served the Federal Communications Commission for over twenty-five years. During that time he was its Chief of Branch in the International Division of the Common Carrier Bureau, an administrative law judge, and Chief of the Office of Satellite Communications. Most recently, he served as Deputy Chief of the Common Carrier Bureau and as Director of the Special Staff for the AT&T proceeding.

Barbara B. Murray has taught at the College of Business and Administration at the University of Detroit since 1967. She has also served as a consultant to several governmental and educational institutions and as an expert witness for a number of corporations.

About the Editors

Werner Sichel is professor of economics at Western Michigan University. He received the B.S. at New York University, and the M.A. and Ph.D. in economics at Northwestern University. The author of a recent text, *Basic Economic Concepts,* he has also contributed a number of books and articles in the areas of antitrust policy, patent policy, conglomerate mergers and acquisitions, economic concentration, oligopoly theory, and business reciprocity. He has served as a consultant to several corporations, especially on patent policy. While Fulbright-Hays Senior Lecturer at the University of Belgrade, he pursued a research interest in the Yugoslavian economy. Currently he is President of the Economics Society of Michigan.

Thomas G. Gies is professor of finance at the University of Michigan, Ann Arbor. He received the B.A., the M.A., and the Ph.D. from the University of Michigan. Former president of the Midwest Finance Association (1971-72), Dr. Gies was also Director of the Financial Management Association (1973). He is the author of several books, the most recent being *Regulation in Further Perspective* (Ballinger, 1974). In addition Dr. Gies has contributed to various business and finance journals.